Bloom's Modern Critical Interpretations

Bloom's Modern Critical Interpretations

Bloom's Modern Critical Interpretations

Arthur Miller's
Death of a Salesman
Updated Edition

Edited and with an introduction by
Harold Bloom
Sterling Professor of the Humanities
Yale University

CHELSEA HOUSE
PUBLISHERS
An imprint of Infobase Publishing

Bloom's Modern Critical Interpretations: Death of a Salesman, Updated Edition

©2007 Infobase Publishing

Introduction © 2007 by Harold Bloom

Chelsea House
An imprint of Infobase Publishing
132 West 31st Street
New York NY 10001

Library of Congress Cataloging-in-Publication Data
Arthur Miller's Death of a salesman / Harold Bloom, editor. — Updated ed.
    p. cm.
  Includes bibliographical references and index.
  ISBN 0-7910-9302-6
 1. Miller, Arthur, 1915-2005. Death of a salesman.
I. Bloom, Harold. II. Title: Death of a salesman.
  PS3525.I5156D433 2006
  812'.52—dc22   2006015137

Chelsea House books are available at special discounts when purchased in bulk quantities for businesses, associations, institutions, or sales promotions. Please call our Special Sales Department in New York at (212) 967-8800 or (800) 322-8755.

You can find Chelsea House on the World Wide Web at http://www.chelseahouse.com

Contributing Editor: Pamela Loos
Cover designed by Ben Peterson
Cover photo © Hulton Archive/Getty Images

Printed in the United States of America
Bang EJB 10 9 8 7 6 5 4 3 2 1

This book is printed on acid-free paper.

All links and web addresses were checked and verified to be correct at the time of publication. Because of the dynamic nature of the web, some addresses and links may have changed since publication and may no longer be valid.

Contents

Editor's Note

My Introduction acknowledges Miller's limitations as a writer, while I attempt to define how *Death of a Salesman* nevertheless achieves aesthetic dignity.

The gifted German-Jewish critic Peter Szondi illuminates Miller's swerve away from Ibsen into the realm of memory, while Leah Hadomi examines father-son relations in the play and Steven R. Centola meditates upon Miller's affirmation of family ethics.

Miller is praised by Stephen Barker for authentically invoking the Muse of Tragedy, after which Christopher Bigsby grants Miller the eminence of theater poetry.

Colby H. Kullman interviews the dramatist on the golden anniversary of the play, while Frank Ardolino explores Miller's mastery of the vernacular.

Terry Otten tries to find an honorable place for Miller's drama somewhere between high tragedy and mere melodrama after which Fred Ribkoff analyzes the quest for identity in *Death of a Salesman*.

In this volume's final essay, Austin E. Quigley contrasts *Death of a Salesman* with *After the Fall*, composed 15 years later, and confirms what he takes to be Miller's moral authority in each.

My afterthought considers the character of Willy Loman.

HAROLD BLOOM

Introduction

I

Rather like Eugene O'Neill before him, Arthur Miller raises, at least for me, the difficult critical question as to whether there is not an element in drama that is other than literary, even contrary in value (supposed or real) to literary values, perhaps even to aesthetic values. O'Neill, a very nearly great dramatist, particularly in *The Iceman Cometh* and *Long Day's Journey Into Night*, is not a good writer, except perhaps in his stage directions. Miller is by no means a bad writer, but he is scarcely an eloquent master of the language. I have reread *All My Sons*, *Death of a Salesman*, and *The Crucible*, and am compelled to reflect how poorly they reread, though all of them, properly staged, are very effective dramas, and *Death of a Salesman* is considerably more than that. It ranks with *Iceman*, *Long Day's Journey*, Williams's *A Streetcar Named Desire*, Wilder's *The Skin of Our Teeth*, and Albee's *The Zoo Story* as one of the half-dozen crucial American plays. Yet its literary status seems to me somewhat questionable, which returns me to the issue of what there is in drama that can survive indifferent or even poor writing.

Defending *Death of a Salesman*, despite what he admits is a sentimental glibness in its prose, Kenneth Tynan memorably observed: "But the theater is an impure craft, and *Death of a Salesman* organizes its impurities with an emotional effect unrivalled in postwar drama." The observation still seems true, nearly half a century after Tynan made it, yet how unlikely a similar

1

statement would seem if ventured about Ibsen, Miller's prime precursor. Do we speak of *Hedda Gabler* organizing its impurities with an unrivalled emotional effect? Why is the American drama, except for Thornton Wilder (its one great sport), addicted to an organization of impurities, a critical phrase perhaps applicable only to Theodore Dreiser, among the major American novelists? Why is it that we have brought forth *The Scarlet Letter*, *Moby-Dick*, *Adventures of Huckleberry Finn*, *The Portrait of a Lady*, *The Sun Also Rises*, *The Great Gatsby*, *As I Lay Dying*, *Miss Lonelyhearts*, *The Crying of Lot 49*, but no comparable dramas? A nation whose poets include Whitman, Dickinson, Frost, Stevens, Eliot, Hart Crane, Elizabeth Bishop, James Merrill, and John Ashbery, among so many others of the highest aesthetic dignity—how can it offer us only O'Neill, Miller, and Williams as its strongest playwrights?

Drama at its most eminent tends not to appear either too early or too late in any national literature. The United States may be the great exception, since before O'Neill we had little better than Clyde Fitch, and our major dramas (it is to be hoped) have not yet manifested themselves. I have seen little speculation upon this matter, with the grand exception of Alvin B. Kernan, the magisterial scholarly critic of Shakespeare and of Elizabethan dramatic literature. Meditating upon American plays, in 1967, Kernan tuned his initially somber notes to hopeful ones:

> Thus with all our efforts, money, and good intentions, we have not yet achieved a theater; and we have not, I believe, because we do not see life in historic and dramatic terms. Even our greatest novelists and poets, sensitive and subtle though they are, do not think dramatically, and should not be asked to, for they express themselves and us in other forms more suited to their visions (and ours). But we have come very close at moments to having great plays, if not a great theatrical tradition. When the Tyrone family stands in its parlor looking at the mad mother holding her wedding dress and knowing that all the good will in the world cannot undo what the past has done to them; when Willy Loman, the salesman, plunges again and again into the past to search for the point where it all went irremediably wrong and cannot find any one fatal turning point; when the Antrobus family, to end on a more cheerful note, drafts stage hands from backstage to take the place of sick actors, gathers its feeble and ever-disappointed hopes, puts its miserable home together again after another in a series of unending disasters stretching from the ice age to the present; then we are very close to accepting our entanglement in

the historical process and our status as actors, which may in time produce a true theater.

That time has not yet come, but I think that Kernan was more right even than he knew. Our greatest novelists and poets continue not to see life in historic and dramatic terms, precisely because our literary tradition remains incurably Emersonian, and Emerson shrewdly dismissed both history and drama as European rather than American. An overtly anti-Emersonian poet-novelist like Robert Penn Warren does see life in historic and dramatic terms, and yet has done his best work away from the stage, despite his effort to write *All the King's Men* as a play. Our foremost novelist, Henry James, failed as a dramatist, precisely because he was more Emersonian than he knew, and turned too far inward in nuanced vision for a play to be his proper mode of representation. One hardly sees Faulkner or Frost, Hemingway or Stevens as dramatists, though they all made their attempts. Nor would a comparison of *The Waste Land* and *The Family Reunion* be kind to Eliot's dramatic ambitions. The American literary mode, whether narrative or lyric, tends towards romance and rumination, or fantastic vision, rather than drama. Emerson, genius of the shores of America, directed us away from history, and distrusted drama as a revel. Nothing is got for nothing; Faulkner and Wallace Stevens, aesthetic light-years beyond O'Neill and Tennessee Williams, seem to mark the limits of the literary imagination in our American century. It is unfair to *All My Sons* and *Death of a Salesman* to read them with the high expectations we rightly bring to *As I Lay Dying* and *Notes Toward a Supreme Fiction*. Miller, a social dramatist, keenly aware of history, fills an authentic American need, certainly for his own time.

II

The strength of *Death of a Salesman* may be puzzling, and yet is beyond dispute; the continued vitality of the play cannot be questioned. Whether it has the aesthetic dignity of tragedy is not clear, but no other American play is worthier of the term, so far. I myself resist the drama each time I reread it, because it seems that its language will not hold me, and then I see it played on stage, and I yield to it. Miller has caught an American kind of suffering that is also a universal mode of pain, quite possibly because his hidden paradigm for his American tragedy is an ancient Jewish one. Willy Loman is hardly a biblical figure, and he is not supposed to be Jewish, yet something crucial in him is Jewish, and the play does belong to that undefined entity we can call Jewish literature, just as Pinter's *The Caretaker* rather surprisingly does. The only meaning of Willy Loman is the pain he suffers, and the pain his fate causes us to suffer. His tragedy makes sense only in the Freudian world of repression, which happens also to be the world of normative Jewish memory. It is a world in which everything has already happened, in which there never can be anything new again, because there is total sense or meaningfulness in everything, which is to say, in which everything hurts.

That cosmos informed by Jewish memory is the secret strength or permanent coherence of *Death of a Salesman*, and accounts for its ability to withstand the shrewd critique of Eric Bentley, who found that the genres of tragedy and of social drama destroyed one another here. Miller's passionate insistence upon tragedy is partly justified by Willy's perpetual sense of being in exile. Commenting on his play, Miller wrote that: "The truly valueless man, a man without ideals, is always perfectly at home anywhere." But Willy, in his own small but valid way, has his own version of the Nietzschean "desire to be elsewhere, the desire to be different," and it does reduce to a Jewish version. Doubtless, as Mary McCarthy first noted, Willy "could not be Jewish because he had to be American." Nearly sixty years later, that distinction is pragmatically blurred, and we can wonder if the play might be stronger if Willy were more overtly Jewish.

We first hear Willy say: "It's all right. I came back." His last utterance is the mere repetition of the desperately hushing syllable: "Shhh!" just before he rushes out to destroy himself. A survivor who no longer desires to survive is something other than a tragic figure. Willy, hardly a figure of capable imagination, nevertheless is a representation of terrible pathos. Can we define precisely what that pathos is?

Probably the most famous speech in *Death of a Salesman* is Linda's pre-elegy for her husband, of whom she is soon to remark: "A small man can be just as exhausted as a great man." The plangency of Linda's lament has a universal poignancy, even if we wince at its naked design upon us:

> Willy Loman never made a lot of money. His name was never in the paper. He's not the finest character that ever lived. But he's a human being, and a terrible thing is happening to him. So attention must be paid. He's not to be allowed to fall into his grave like an old dog. Attention, attention must be finally paid to such a person.

Behind this is Miller's belated insistence "that everyone knew Willy Loman," which is a flawed emphasis on Miller's part, since he first thought of calling the play *The Inside of His Head*, and Willy already lives in a phantasmagoria when the drama opens. You cannot know a man half lost in the American dream, a man who is unable to tell past from present. Perhaps the play should have been called *The Dying of a Salesman*, because Willy is dying throughout. That is the pathos of Linda's passionate injunction that attention must be finally paid to such a person, a human being to whom a terrible thing is happening. Nothing finds Willy anymore; everything loses him. He is a man upon whom the sun has gone down, to appropriate a great phrase from Ezra Pound. But have we defined as yet what is particular about his pathos?

I think not. Miller, a passionate moralist, all but rabbinical in his ethical vision, insists upon giving us Willy's, and his sons', sexual infidelities as synecdoches of the failure of Willy's vision of reality. Presumably, Willy's sense of failure, his belief that he has no right to his wife, despite Linda's love for him, is what motivates Willy's deceptions, and those of his sons after him. Yet Willy is not destroyed by his sense of failure. Miller may be a better interpreter of Miller than he is a dramatist. I find it wholly persuasive that Willy is destroyed by love, by his sudden awareness that his son Biff truly loves him. Miller beautifully comments that Willy resolves to die when "he is given his existence ... his fatherhood, for which he has always striven and which until now he could not achieve." That evidently is the precise and terrible pathos of Willy's character and of his fate. He is a good man, who wants only to earn and to deserve the love of his wife and of his sons. He is self-slain, not by the salesman's dream of America, but by the universal desire to be loved by one's own, and to be loved beyond what one believes one deserves. Miller is not one of the masters of metaphor, but in *Death of a Salesman* he memorably achieves a pathos that none of us would be wise to dismiss.

PETER SZONDI

Memory: Miller

$\mathbf{A}$rthur Miller's evolution from imitator to innovator, which occurred between the publication of his first two works, is the clearest example of that general change in style that both unites and separates the turn-of-the-century dramatists and those of the present: the emergence out of dramatic form of a new formal structure for those epic elements that had previously only been given thematic expression. If this process, which is central to the developmental history of the modern theater, has, up to this point, been presented mainly in terms of a comparison between the two periods—by contrasting Ibsen and Pirandello, Chekhov and Wilder, Hauptmann and Brecht—in Miller's case, as with Strindberg's earlier, it can be illuminated by the works of a single author.

In *All My Sons* (1947), Miller tried to preserve Ibsen's analytical approach to social dramaturgy by transferring it into the American present. An inexorable analysis slowly reveals the long-hidden crime committed by the head of the Keller family: his delivery of defective airplane parts to the Army, a deed that involves him in another—the suicide of his son Larry— which has also been kept secret. All the secondary aspects of the action needed to narrate the past as a dramatic event are at hand—the return of Larry's former fiancée and her brother, for example. Their father, an employee of Keller's, was wrongfully imprisoned for Keller's offense. Even

From *Theory of the Modern Drama*, edited and translated by Michael Hays. © 1987 by the University of Minnesota.

Ibsen's often heavy-handed use of the set is preserved in this work: an element of the decor gives visible presence to the ongoing internal effects of the past, while also laboring to symbolize the deeper meaning of the play. In this case it is the tree that long ago had been planted for Larry. Felled by the previous night's storm, its shattered stump stands in the backyard where the play is set. If *All My Sons* had not been followed by *Death of a Salesman*, it might possibly have been discussed here as an example of Ibsen's powerful influence in the Anglo-Saxon world, an influence that begins with G[eorge] B[ernard] Shaw and lives on today. As it is, however, the play can be regarded as a work from his apprentice years, as if Miller, engaged in giving scenic form to a "wasted lifetime"[1] and in particular to a traumatic past, had, while following in Ibsen's footsteps, come to understand the manner in which dramatic form resists this thematic and the costs attached to making the former serve the latter. What was shown here earlier with respect to *John Gabriel Borkman* must have become clear to Miller as he worked on *All My Sons*: the contradiction between a remembered past conveyed by the thematic and the spatial-temporal present postulated by dramatic form; the resulting need to contrive a supplementary action with which to motivate the analysis; and, the disharmony produced by the fact that this second set of events dominates the stage while the real "action" emerges only in the confessions of the characters.

In his second play, Miller tries to escape these contradictions by surrendering dramatic form. Fundamental here is the fact that he does not disguise the analysis as action. The past is no longer forced into open discussion by a dramatic conflict; the dramatis personae are no longer portrayed as masters of the past to satisfy a formal principle when in fact they are its helpless victims. Instead, the past achieves representation in the same way that it emerges in life itself—of its own accord, in the *mémoire involontaire* (Proust). Therefore, the past remains a subjective experience and can create no illusory bridges between the individuals whom the analysis brings together—individuals whom it had left in lifelong separation. Thus, instead of an interpersonal action that would call forth discussion of the past, the present generated by the thematic discloses the psychic state of the individual overpowered by memory. Willy Loman, an aging salesman, is presented in this manner; the play begins as he slips completely under the thrall of memory. The family has recently begun to notice that he talks to himself. In fact, he is actually talking to them, not in the real present but in the past he remembers, which no longer leaves him alone. The present of the play is constituted by the forty-eight hours that follow Loman's unexpected return from a business trip. The past had continuously gotten the better of him as he sat behind the steering wheel of his car. He tries in vain to arrange a transfer to the New York office of the company he has represented for several decades; his constant references to the past reveal the state he is in, and he is fired. Finally, Loman commits suicide so that his family can benefit from his insurance policy.

This actional framework, which is situated in the present, has little to do with that found in Ibsen's Drama or even in *All My Sons*. It is not a dramatic event that closes on itself; and it does not require that the past be conjured up in dialogue. The scene between Loman and his employer is characteristic in this respect. The latter is unwilling to join in a conversation that would give presence to the salesman's career and to his own father, who is supposed to have been favorably disposed toward Loman. He finds an excuse to leave the room and hurries out, leaving Loman alone with his ever more vivid memories.

These memories in turn create a means (one already long familiar to the cinema under the name flashback) of introducing the past into the space beyond dialogue. The scene shifts constantly in the play staged for Loman by his *mémoire involontaire*. Unlike the Ibsenesque courtroom procedure, remembrance occurs without being spoken of—that is, entirely on the level of form.[2] The protagonist regards himself in the past and, as self-remembering *I*, is absorbed into the formal subjectivity of the work. The scene presents only the epic object of this subjectivity, the remembered *I* itself, the salesman in the past, his conversations with the members of his family. The latter are no longer independent dramatis personae; they emerge as references to the central *I*, in the same manner as do the character projections in expressionist dramaturgy. One can readily grasp the epic nature of this play of memory by comparing it to the "play within a play" as it appears in the Drama. Hamlet's play, which presents the imagined past in order to "catch the conscience of the king,"[3] is built into the action in the form of an episode. It constitutes a closed sphere that leaves the surrounding world of action intact. Because this second play is a thematic piece that does not need to conceal the fact of its performance, the time and place of the two actions are not in conflict—the dramatic unities and the absoluteness of the events are maintained. In *Death of a Salesman*, on the other hand, the past is not played as a thematic episode; the present and its action constantly overflow into the play of the past. No troupe of actors enters; without saying a word, the characters can become actors enacting themselves because the alternation between immediate/personal and past/remembered events is anchored in the epic principle of form operative here. The dramatic unities are likewise abolished—indeed, abolished in the most radical sense: memory signifies not only a multiplicity of times and places but also the absolute loss of their identity. The temporal-spatial present of the action is not simply relativized in terms of other presents; on the contrary, it is in itself relative. Therefore, there is no real change in the setting, and, at the same time, it is perpetually transformed. The salesman's house remains on stage, but in the scenes remembered, its walls are of no concern—as is the case with memory, which has no temporal or spatial limits. This relativity of the present becomes particularly clear in those transitional scenes that belong to the outer as well as the inner reality. Such is the situation in the first act when the memory figure, Ben, Willy's brother, appears on stage while he and his neighbor, Charley, are playing cards:

> *Willy*: I'm awfully tired Ben.
> *Charley*: Good, keep playing; you'll sleep better. Did you call me Ben?
> *Willy*: That's funny. For a second there you reminded me of my brother Ben.[4]

The salesman says nothing that indicates he sees his dead brother in front of him. His appearance could be a hallucination, but only within dramatic form, which by definition excludes the inner world. Yet, in this play, present reality and the reality of the past achieve simultaneous representation. Because Loman is reminded of his brother, the latter appears on stage: memory has been incorporated into the principle underlying scenic form. Because interior monologue (dialogue with a figure evoked by memory), stands side by side with dialogue, the result is a Chekhovian speaking at cross purposes:

> *Ben*: Is Mother living with you?
> *Willy*: No, she died a long time ago.
> *Charley*: Who?
> *Ben*: That's too bad. Fine specimen of a lady, Mother.
> *Willy (to Charley)*: Heh?
> *Ben*: I'd hoped to see the old girl.
> *Charley*: Who died?
> *Ben*: Heard anything from Father, have you?
> *Willy (unnerved)*: What do you mean, who died?
> *Charley*: ... What're you talkin' about?[5]

To give dramatic form to this sort of continual misunderstanding, Chekhov needed the supporting theme supplied by deafness.[6] In *Death of a Salesman*, on the other hand, it arises formally out of the side-by-side existence of the two worlds. Their concurrent representation sets in motion the new principle of form. Its advantage over the Chekhovian technique is obvious. The supporting theme, the symbolic character of which remains vague, does introduce the possibility of mutual misunderstanding, but it also hides the real source of this misunderstanding—the individual's preoccupation with himself and with a remembered past, a past that can appear as such only after the formal principle of the Drama is abolished.

It is this past, once again present, that finally opens the salesman's eyes as he desperately tries to understand his own misfortune and, even more, the failed career of his elder son [Biff]. While sitting across from his sons in a restaurant, a scene from the past suddenly surfaces in his memory and, therefore, becomes visible to the audience as well: his son finds him in a Boston hotel room with his mistress. At this point, Loman can understand why his son later wandered from job to job and why he thwarted his career prospects by stealing: he wanted to punish his father.

In *Death of a Salesman*, Miller did not want to reveal this secret, the failure of the father (which was borrowed from Ibsen and central to *All My Sons*), through a judicial procedure invented for the sake of form. He gave credence to Balzac's comment, under the sign of which both Ibsen's and Miller's characters stand: "We all die unknown."[7] Because memory takes its place beside the (always) present of the dialogue, which constitutes the sole representational possibility of the Drama, the play successfully presents a dramatic paradox: the past of a number of characters is given visible presence but only for a single consciousness. In contrast to the analysis that is part of the thematic in Ibsen, this play of the past, founded on the principle of form, has no effect on the other characters. For the son, this scene remains a permanent and heavily guarded secret. He is unable to reveal to anyone the shattering effect it has had on has life. Because of this, his mute hatred breaks into the open neither before his father's suicide nor after it. And in the "Requiem," which closes the play, it is precisely the unsuspecting quality of the remarks made by Linda, the salesman's wife, that makes them so moving.

> *Linda*: Forgive me, dear. I can't cry, I don't know what it is, but I can't cry. I don't understand it. Why did you ever do that? Help me, Willy, I can't cry. It seems to me that you're just on another trip. I keep expecting you. Willy, dear, I can't cry. Why did you do it? I search and I search and I search, and I can't understand it....
>
> *The Curtain Falls*[8]

NOTES

1. See p. 16.
2. See pp. 47–48,
3. Act II, scene 2.

4. Miller, *Death of a Salesman* (London, 1952) [pp. 44–45]. [All citations in this translation are from the Viking edition (New York, 1958).]

5. Ibid., p. 46.

6. See p. 21f.

7. See p. 17.

8. *Death of a Salesman*, p. 139. [Closing lines not cited.]

LEAH HADOMI

Rhythm Between Fathers and Sons:
Death of a Salesman

"THE INSIDE OF HIS HEAD"

The returning son in *Death of a Salesman* is Biff, who left home and
became a "one dollar man". His return home, not, we note, for the first time,
intensifies a continuous family crisis focusing on Willy, the father, as the
protagonist of the play. Homecoming and its effects are a recurrent situation,
and the final homecoming is dramatized as the climax of a lengthy,
complicated inner process. The deep and disturbing relationship between
father and returning son is doubled with another meaningful father–son
relationship, between Willy as a son and the father figure to whom he relates
affectively. The relationship between Biff and his father revolves around
misunderstanding and "guilt"; that between Willy and his father takes place
wholly in the realm of fantasy. There is a similar doubling of brother
relationships: the ambiguous relationship between Biff and Happy and the
tie between Willy and his brother Ben in the former's fantasy world. In both
relationships, the son who left arouses envy in the son who stayed. This
double set of father/son and brother/brother relationships emphasises the
aspects of the archi-pattern in this drama, and the effect is achieved by
focusing on Willy's inner life. This inner life is peopled by characters who are
effectively a "cast of ideals".

From *The Homecoming Theme in Modern Drama: The Return of the Prodigal.* © 1992 by the Edwin
Mellen Press.

At his father's grave Biff sums up Willy's life thus: "He had the wrong dreams. All, all wrong" (p. 222). Biff, in his belated understanding of his father, recognizes Willy's dreamlike ideals but regards them as false. Miller himself explained:

> The trouble with Willy Loman is that he has tremendously powerful ideals ... [the play's aim is] to set forth what happens when a man does not have a grip on the forces of life and has no sense of values which will lead him to that kind of a grip.[1]

This statement by the playwright emphasises the gap between adherence to ideals and the ability to function successfully in real life.

Biff is the only character in the play who understands the importance of Willy's inability to find the "right dream", and that his life was, for him, a torment. It is to Biff, the returning son, to whom Willy relates most affectively. The function of the returning son is linked to the father's value-orientation and ideals, which are both embodied in his fantasy, his memories, and his expectations of himself and of others. Willy not only tries, albeit unsuccessfully, to live up to his own moral code, he also judges everyone around him by that code. It is most painful to him to see Biff falling short of his ideals. Biff's reappearance evokes Willy's reminiscences as well as his self-expectations as son, brother and father. The subtitle of *Death of a Salesman*, *Certain Private Conversations in Two Acts and a Requiem*, as well as the title originally considered by the playwright, *The Inside of His Head*, already point to the play's thematic essence and major formal characteristic.[2] Thematically, Miller's drama deals with the tension between the protagonist's private inner world and external reality. Its principal structural characteristic consists of the integration of dramatic realism and expressionism.[3]

The conflicting inner selves that make up Willy Loman's many-sided persona represent his experience of the outer world refracted through the distorting medium of his fantasies. As the action of the play progresses, the connections between Willy's inner world and external reality, which are tenuous enough to begin with, grow increasingly unstable and volatile. He is driven to kill himself, the ultimate act of self-deception in his struggle to impose his fantasies upon a reality that consistently thwarts his ambitions and will.[4]

The shifts in Willy Loman's mind between his dreams and actuality, on the level of his personal existence, and between fantasy and realism on the level of dramatic presentation, are conveyed in structural terms by the patterns in which the play's formal elements unfold to establish its dramatic rhythm. In the following analysis of Miller's play, we will take our cue from the conceptions of dramatic rhythm as set out by Paul M. Levitt and

Kathleen George.[5] This analysis will show how much the rhythm of the play reinforces the "doubled" father/son and brother/brother relationships within it.

Not only is Willy Loman the chief character but it is primarily from his inner perspective that the play's dramatic action derives its meaning. The actual events enacted in his presence, particularly the return of his son Biff, become the trigger for Willy's recollections and fantasies which constitute the play's imaginary sequences. The significance of each of the play's episodes, as well as the structure of the plot as a whole, depends on the rhythmic alternations between actuality and Willy's mental responses to them. His ideal self-image and the reality of his actual behaviour and circumstances are the poles of both his inner existence and his dramatic interactions with the other characters. The personalities of each of the *dramatis personae* are connected specifically with a particular feature of Willy's inner self, with, a particular stance he has adopted towards his environment, or with one of the values to which he has educated his sons. The conduct of the play's other characters is in great measure both the effect of his illusory perception of external reality and the cause of his deepening submersion into the world of his fantasies. When reality becomes too painful, Willy retreats into a dream world, consisting of his roseate recollections of the past and of fantasies in which he fulfils the aspirations, the attainment of which has eluded him in life.[6] Although his memories are based on actual events, these are falsified in his mind by wishful thinking about how they ought to have turned out. Hence in Willy's mind, reality as it is immediately experienced by him merges in his consciousness with his recollection of distant events to form a seamless continuum of past and present time.

Willy is torn between his need, on the one hand, to give expression to his innermost longings by establishing a direct and harmonious connection with nature and by manual labour; on the other, he wishes to maintain his place in society by creating a facade of emulous and combative self-assertiveness, which he tries to reconcile with his obsessive and desperate need to be admired and loved by others.[7] Together these contrary tendencies account for the conflicts both in his ideal conception of himself and in the way he conceives of others, in relation to the idealized image of his own personality. Moreover, Willy's ideal self-image is as fragmented as his real personality. Rather than consisting of a single coherent self, it is compacted of a number of contradictory selves, each of which might alone have formed the core of an integrated personality relatively free of tension, but which together make up an unstable persona that ultimately costs the protagonist his life.

Willy Loman spends much of his time on stage in an ongoing inner dialogue with a number of characters. Some, like Willy's son and his friend Charley, belong to the immediate and concrete reality which is being dramatized. The other figures emerge from Willy's recollections of the past and animate his inner world: his father, his older brother Ben, and old Dave Singleman. All three figures owe their presentation and description in the play to Willy's imagination, whose creation they essentially are. The characters that live through Willy's imagination are both the fruit and inspiration of this inner existence; and, by virtue of Willy Loman's function as the protagonist from whose perspective much of the play's action is seen, these characters furnish the focus of the clash of fantasy and reality in both Willy himself and the other *dramatis personae* of the play.

In Willy's consciousness each of the three men from the past has assumed the status of a personal hero and exemplar whom he aspires to emulate. Together they may constitute the end of the continuum between the ideal and the actual along which Willy's fluctuations between fantasy and reality take place. Each in his own right also furnishes Willy with a separate "ego ideal" that occupies a distinct place on a descending scale of proximity to the real world.[8]

Connected with Willy's past is the memory of his own father, who never assumes substantial form in Willy's mind but nonetheless powerfully informs his fantasy, primarily through his imagined conversations with Ben. Willy's father, the least accessible and most dimly remembered of the protagonist's exemplars, functions as his "absolute" ego ideal. His brother, Ben, against whose adventurous life and grand mercantile enterprises in far-off places Willy measures his own inadequacy and petty destiny, is his "desiderative" ego ideal. And last, Dave Singleman, the quintessence of the successful salesman and Willy's inspiration and model for feasible achievement, serves as the protagonist's "attainable" ego ideal.

Of these three ideal figures, Willy's father is the most remote from actuality and belongs to the very earliest and vaguest childhood recollections. Though not one of the *dramatis personae*, and only spoken of twice in the course of the play—during Ben's first "visitation" in Act One (pp. 156–57), and then briefly, by Willy, in Howard's office in Act Two (p. 180), his spirit dogs Willy and is repeatedly referred to on an auditory level by the sound of flute music. This is first heard as a sort of signature tune when the curtain goes up on the play, and is last heard when the curtain falls on the "Requiem". Hearing his father play the flute is about the only sensory memory Willy has of him—that and his father's "big beard". What we know of the picture in Willy's mind of the man, we learn from the description he receives from Ben's apparition. And what emerges from Ben's account is a part-mythical, part-allegorical figure. The image of him drawn by Ben is an emblematic composite of the classic types that are representative of America's heroic age: Willy's father is at once the untamed natural man and the westward-bound pioneer, the artisan, the great inventor, and the successful entrepreneur.

Willy's brother Ben represents an ideal which is closer to reality, that of worldly success, though on a scale so exalted as to be utterly beyond Willy's reach. To Willy's mind, Ben is the personification of the great American virtues of self-reliance and initiative by which an enterprising man may attain untold wealth; and it is through Ben that Willy tries to maintain personal connection with the myth of the individual's triumphant march from rags to riches.

In Willy's consciousness, Ben mediates between the domains of the ideal and the real. The aura of legend is nearly as strong in his brother as it is in his father. He, too, is a journeyer and adventurer. But what animates him in his travels appears to be less a hankering for the open road and the "grand outdoors" than the idea of the fortune to be made there. Sentiment plays no part in the tough maxims he tosses out to account for his success. Nor does he let family feeling cloud his purpose or divert him from his quest for riches, as is evident from the ease with which he abandons his search for his father to pursue diamond wealth in Africa or in the offhand manner in which he receives news of his mother's death. Even Willy gets short shrift from his older brother. Nevertheless, it is Ben's qualities of toughness, unscrupulousness, and implacability in the pursuit of gain that Willy wishes for himself and wants his boys to acquire.

Of Willy Loman's three personal heroes, Dave Singleman stands in the most immediate relation to the actuality of Willy's life. Neither the ideal of natural manhood personified by Willy's father nor the incarnation of freebooting enterprise embodied by his brother, Singleman represents success that is attainable. In Singleman the concept of success is cut down to Willy's size, reduced to an idea more nearly within his scope, that of getting ahead by being "well liked". Success as exemplified by Dave Singleman serves, as well, to sustain in Willy the feeling; that though lacking in the daring and toughness that his father passed on to Ben, he too possesses an essential prerequisite for material achievement, one that he can bequeath to his own sons. So, poised in Howard's office between the phantoms of his dead brother and of Biff in his teens, Willy proclaims in an excess of confidence: "It's who you know and the smile on your face! It's contacts, Ben, contacts!" (p. 184).

Willy is not content merely to admire these men. He also internalizes their qualities and the ideas they represent, diminished and trivialising them in the process. The ideas of being in close touch with nature and taking to the open road that are inspired by Willy's memory of his father are reduced in his own life to puttering about in the back yard of his suburban Brooklyn home and making his routine rounds as a travelling salesman; the idea of venturesome private enterprise for high stakes represented by his brother depreciates to drumming merchandise for a commission; and even the example of Singleman's being "remembered and loved and helped by so many different people" (p. 180), over which Willy rhapsodises to Howard Wagner, is degraded in his own aspirations to the condition of being merely popular and well-liked.

Three of the characters among the principal *dramatis personae* of the play, Biff, Happy, and Charley, function in the real world as analogous to the ideal types in Willy's consciousness. Although none of them is a complete substantiation of Willy's ego ideals, each character has a dominant trait that identifies him with either Willy's father, or Ben, or Dave Singleman, and which determines Willy's relationship with him.

Biff, the returning son, most closely resembles his grandfather in rejecting the constraints imposed by the middle-class routines of holding down a job and making a living, and in his preference for the life of a drifter out West, working as a hired farmhand outdoors. He has a strong touch of the artist and dreamer in his temperament. He is also the most complex character of the three, the most at odds with himself. In this he closely resembles Willy. Like his father, Biff is torn between rural nostalgia and his need for solid achievement, and is tormented by the knowledge of personal failure. "I've always made a point of not wasting my life", he tells Happy, and then confesses to him, "and everytime I come back here I know that all I've done is to waste my life" (p. 139).

Happy corresponds to Ben, if only in a meagre and debased way. He shares his uncle's unscrupulousness and amorality, but has little of his singleness of purpose; and what he has of the last he dedicates to cuckolding his superiors at work and to the pursuit of women in general, activities that make up the only field in which he excels, as Linda recognizes when she sums him up as a "philandering bum" (p. 163). He also resembles Ben in the shallowness of his filial emotions. The trite praise he bestows on Linda— "What a woman! They broke the mold when they made her" (p. 169)—is on its own vulgar level as perfunctory and unfeeling as Ben's more elegantly phrased endorsement, "Fine specimen of a lady, Mother" (p. 155). However, some of his traits remind us of Willy, such as his bluster and nursing of injured pride, his insecurity about making good, as well as his philandering.

Charley is Dave Singleman brought down to earth. He has none of Singleman's flamboyance. Rather, his is a successful salesmanship domesticated. Singleman worked out of a hotel room. Charley maintains an office with a secretary and an accountant. He is stolid but honest and decent, and though not loved like Singleman, he is respected. And, by Willy's own startled admission towards the end, he is Willy Loman's only friend. He is also Willy's perfect foil, a man at peace with what he is and his place in the world.[9]

Except for Charley, the principal characters of *Death of a Salesman* share the same condition of being torn between the conflicting claims of ideality and actuality; and in this capacity the interrelations between them serve to extend and reinforce the rhythmic articulation of the play on a variety of formal levels. Among the consequences of the inner conflicts and contradictions of Willy Loman and his sons are their uncertainty and confusion concerning their own identities, admitted by each at some point in the play. Biff reveals to his mother, "I just can't take hold, Mom. I can't take hold of some kind of a life" (p. 161); Happy tells Biff, "I don't know what the hell I'm workin' for. And still, goddamit, I'm lonely" (p. 139); and Willy confesses to Ben, "I still feel—kind of temporary about myself" (p. 159).[10]

Willy Loman's attitude to the real characters of the play is determined by their relation to the corresponding ideal types in his mind. None of the real characters is an unalloyed embodiment of these exemplars, who have all been debased to varying degrees in their corporeal counterparts. For example, Willy's most complex and ambivalent relationship is with Biff, who is associated most closely with Willy's absolute ego ideal.[11] It is of his older, "prodigal" son that Willy had always expected the most, and it is Biff's failure to live up to his expectations that grieves him the most. By comparison, his relationship with Happy, of whom he expects much less, is straightforward and indifferent. Willy's relationship with Charley is also determined by Charley's proximity to the ideal and his own distance from it. Because Charley comes the closest of everyone Willy knows to the attainable ideal he has set himself but failed to achieve, he treats him with a mixture of respect and envy. This is what prevents Willy from accepting Charley's offer of a job, because doing so would be tantamount to an admission of failure, a reason never stated explicitly by Willy but which Charley recognizes, as we learn during Willy's visit to Charley's office in the second act (p. 192):

> Charley: What're you, jealous of me?
> Willy: I can't work for you, that's all, don't ask me why.
> Charley: (*Angered, takes out more bills*) You been jealous of me all your life, you damned fool! Here, pay your insurance.

By taking money from Charley instead, in the guise of a loan, Willy is able both to retain his self-esteem and to cling to his self-delusions. In a rare moment of candour, Willy privately acknowledges Charley's virtues and superiority to himself: "a man of few words, and they respect him" (p. 149); but for the most part he seeks to establish his own pre-eminence by belittling and hectoring him in petty ways, reminding Charley of his ignorance and inadequacy in ordinary matters: domestic repairs, diet, clothing, sports, cards, and so on.

To sum up, therefore, the function of all the principal characters in the play (apart from Linda) is determined by the operation of Willy's consciousness, suspended between reality and dreams. The measure of their moral significance to Willy is contingent on how far they have taken root in the ideal realm of his consciousness; and the extent to which they have done so is in inverse proportion to their actual presence in the dramatic sequences that take place in current time and space. Willy's father, the absolute ideal figure of the play, assumes the status of a recognizable personality only through the account of him received from the shade of his deceased brother in a scene that unfolds entirely in the mind of the protagonist. Otherwise, he is mentioned only once in the real action of the play, when Willy offhandedly refers to him as a prelude to his pathetic boast to Howard, "We've got quite a streak of self-reliance in our family" (p. 180). Ben's name too is hardly mentioned, and then only in passing, in the real dialogue of the play, and it is only in the fantasising episodes that he assumes palpable shape as a character. And finally Dave Singleman, who serves Willy as a tangible, if illusory, example of success potentially within his grasp, comes alive in a present dramatic sequence of the play, even if only through the agency of words rather than personification. Significantly, the short eulogy to him that Willy delivers, and through which Singleman assumes dramatic life, comes at the moment when Willy is about to be fired and thereby deprived of the last vestige of hope for the attainable success Singleman represented.

The rhythm of the sequence of the two episodes focusing on sexual relations (the Boston woman and the restaurant scene where the boys pick up two women) is also a formal means serving a thematic idea.[12] The significance of the "Boston woman" is foreshadowed in Act One but also receives full dramatic revelation in the "restaurant scene" in Act Two, when it is reconstructed orally and visually so as to show its significance in the wider context of Willy's and Biff's relationship and their recognition of what is true and what is false in their lives.[13] Whereas in the Boston scene it is the son who fails in social competition by flunking his test in mathematics, in the restaurant scene both father and son appear equally defeated in the economic and social struggle; and while in the Boston episode Biff, appalled by Willy's infidelity, realizes that his talkative, pretentious father is ineffectual (p. 207) and calls him a "phony little fake" (p. 208), in the restaurant scene Biff confesses to his father the pretensions and illusions of his own life too. Happy's aggressive promiscuity is one other aspect of his latent "jungle" lifestyle. He recognizes that his repeated, almost compulsive affairs with women related to higher executives at his work are an aspect of his "overdeveloped sense of competition" (p. 141). Thus, sexual infidelity is related to the tension between father and son and to the relationship between brother and brother.

The dramatic rhythm of *Death of a Salesman*, as manifested in the development of character, takes place through a complex interplay on the function of *dramatis personae* and their interplay with the three levels of Willy's consciousness: first, on the level of ideality; second on the level of fantasies and dreams; and last, on the level of his perception of concrete reality. It is from these three levels of consciousness that the protagonist's three ego ideals, the absolute, the desiderative, and the attainable, emerge. Taken as a whole, Willy's three levels of consciousness dramatize his attitude to himself, to the others and to social reality.

A number of verbal references, which are also translated into stage effects, have symbolic significance and recur throughout the text of Miller's play. These echo and enhance the play's rhythmic design. Their significance derives from the associations they arouse in the protagonist's consciousness, where they are resolved into two principal symbolic clusters, connected with divergent attitudes that dominate Willy's imaginative life. It is interesting that these can be assigned to "father" and "brother" headings. The first cluster is connected with Willy's deep attachment to nature and his nostalgia for the countryside, feelings whose point of origin can be traced to Willy's father. The major references included in this cluster are to trees, seeds, and "travel" in its broadest sense. The second cluster is associated with commerce and enterprise of the kind personified for Willy by his brother Ben. The chief symbolic references of this cluster are to "jungle", Ben's watch and diamonds.

An evident pattern emerges in the way how the references to trees, wood, branches and leaves bind the domains of fantasy and reality in the play. They are clearly relevant to the ideal figure of Willy's father (a maker of flutes, a musical instrument of wood whose pastoral associations are immediate and altogether obvious), and to Willy's brother Ben (in whose vast tracts of Alaskan timberland Willy almost had a share).

Trees and leaves are the dominant stage effect when Willy's mind turns inward and towards the past, a time when his longings for a rural existence were more nearly satisfied. As he casts his mind back to a time when his home stood in what was still a landscape setting, the large elm trees that had once grown on his property form an important part of his recollections. In the dramatic present, the elms are gone and all that remains of the rural Brooklyn he had known is his backyard, which by the play's end is the setting of Willy's last effort to reassert control over events by planting vegetables in futile defiance of urban encroachment. For Willy, being truly happy means working with tools—"all I'd need would be a little lumber and some peace of mind" (p. 151), he says, hoping for a better future. Trees are involved in his fantasies of Ben's success in the jungle and in the "timberland in Alaska" (p. 183). Trees colour the imagery of Willy's expressions of his inner desperation and need for help, "the woods are burning" (pp. 152, 199). Trees and leaves are thereby involved rhythmically in the linguistic constructs of the play as well as in the visual setting of the stage: the memory of a hammock between the "big trees" (p. 143), of seeds in the garden, of working on the wood ceiling, and the lighting effect of the stage being "covered with leaves" (pp. 142, 151, 200). On the textual level, as well as on the stage, they become signs in the theatrical system indicating the rhythm between fantasy and reality.

Willy's enthusiasm for the outdoors and the countryside is also connected in his mind with the idea of travel and journeying. The idea of travel is inseparable from the images he has of the ideal figures from his past: his father driving his wagon and team of horses across the Western states; Ben globetrotting between continents; and Dave Singleman travelling in the smoker of the New York, New Haven and Hartford line. His own life, too, is inseparable from travel, and the maintenance of the family car is one of his major concerns. His car is essential to him for his livelihood, and it is also the instrument by which he chooses to bring an end to his life. It is the first thematically significant object to appear in the dramatic text of the play, when it is mentioned in a context that foreshadows the manner of Willy's death (p. 132).

The reference to nature is carried over to the second cluster of images bearing on the theme of commerce and enterprise, but now appears in the menacing guise of the "jungle", poles apart from the idyllic associations aroused by the cluster of rural symbols. Its explicit connection with the theme of enterprise and commerce, as well as its association with the attendant idea of aggressive and unscrupulous competition, is fully developed in the presence of all the principal characters in the scene of Ben's first apparition (pp. 154–60). The specific verbal context in which the reference first occurs is twice repeated almost verbatim by Ben: "... when I was seventeen I walked in to the jungle, and when I was twenty-one I walked out. And by God I was rich" (pp. 157, 159–160). On the first occasion when Ben speaks these words he does so at Willy's urging for the benefit of the boys. The second time, is on his departure and they are uttered for Willy's ears alone. What happens between the two utterances brings out the thematic significance of the passage as referring to the rule of the jungle that governs the sort of enterprise that Ben represents. And the event that drives this particular moral home is the sparring match between Ben and Biff, in which Ben departs from the rule of fair play and declaims the precept, "Never fight fair with a stranger, boy. You'll never get out of the jungle that way" (p. 158). By the time Ben's shade departs, Willy seems to have taken Ben's point when he chimes in with great enthusiasm, "That's just the spirit I want to imbue them with! To walk into the jungle! I was right!" (p. 160). But the truth is that Willy was wrong. Ben's lesson is not about going into jungles, but coming out of them, alive and prosperous. The watch and diamond references are associated through Ben with the "jungle" reference. Their connection with one another, and their symbolic bearing on commerce, become obvious once their association with the ideas of time and wealth are established, and we recall that these are proverbially equated in the businessman's adage that time is money.

The watch and diamond references are also merged by a specific object in the play: the "watch fob with a diamond in it" that Ben had given to Willy, and Willy had it pawned to finance Biff's radio correspondence course (p. 160). Thus, time and money, the two cherished commodities of business, are turned in Loman's hands to loss rather than profit.

Willy, as a son, is inwardly completely dependent on the idol of a father he has created, compared to whom all other imagined, idealized figures can only be a reduction. He relates to his own sons according to his own wishful, ideal self-images. On this scale Biff, the returning son, is the focus of Willy's outer aspirations as well as his disappointments. Willy ends his life realising that Biff does love him, but mistakenly rewarding him with "outer" benefits—the life insurance. Biff by now understands his dead father and forgives him his misjudged life. The "sin" here is of a father who could not adjust his inner self to an outward, changing reality. The father, paradoxically, is forgiven by the son, who gains a better understanding of himself.

It is the sin-guilt-innocence aspect of the archi-pattern which is prominent in *Death of a Salesman*. This aspect is transferred to the father figure, Willy, whose frustration over his failure has become part and parcel of the characters and the lives of his failing sons. Both father and sons are "lost". But while the father chooses death as the only way out, the sons, at the end of the play, turn outwards to engage with life in different terms: Happy as "Number One" in the jungle, and Biff as a man who has gained a deeper understanding of his father and of himself.

Biff's real return home is when he is freed from the web of falsehood created by his father's value judgements. His search for identity culminates when he achieves humility through self-knowledge. His return is an extension of Willy's tragic search for himself and for his father in others, as son, brother and father.

Notes

1. "*Death of a Salesman*: a symposium", *Tulane Drama Review*, May 1958, pp. 63–69.
2. See Koon, 1983, p. 13.
3. Parker, 1983, p. 41: "... because the very hesitancies of technique in *Death of a Salesman*, its apparent uncertainty in apportioning realism and expressionism, provide a dramatic excitement".
4. For an extended discussion of the play, see: Hadomi, "Fantasy and Reality: Dramatic Rhythm in *Death of a Salesman*", *Modern Drama* vol. xxxi, 2, June 1988, pp. 157–174.
5. Levitt, 1971; George, 1975. Levitt regards rhythm in theatre to be the creation of two "change producing elements" which he identifies as "recurrence" and "reversal". George observes that dramatic rhythm resides essentially in the "alternation between opposites, generally producing a pattern of tension and relaxation" (p. 9, also pp. 13–16).
6. Strassner, 1980, classifies *Death of a Salesman* as a "memorative drama" (p. 72), in which the memory of the past becomes a trauma which demands even more than an analytical drama like *Ghosts*. For a comparative study of Ibsen's influence on a play by Miller, see: Bronsen, 1968–1969.
7. Jacobson, 1975–1976, p. 249: "His sense of self-value is dependent upon the response of others. Such gestures of recognition provided signals that society, for a period in his life, was a home for him, one where he might hope to make his sons as happily at ease as he".
8. Cf. Parker,: 1983, pp. 43–45; Gordon, 1983, p. 101.
9. Considering the difference between Charley and Willy, Miller, 1965, observes that, unlike Willy: "Charley is not a fanatic ... he has learned to live without that frenzy, that ecstasy of spirit which Willy chases to his end" (p. 37).
10. Bettenhausen, 1972, regards Biff and Happy as extensions of two different aspects of Willy: "In a sense the two sons simply continue the two sides of Willy: Biff, seeing the fragility and even the illusion of the vicarious identity which depends on being well liked in the business world, chooses to accept the challenge of a different destiny. Happy, on the other hand, is captivated by the challenge of the dream and bound to the possibility of success" (p. 201).
11. Cf. Huftel, 1965, p. 108: "[Biff] lives heroic in Willy's mind".
12. Orr, 1981, thinks that Willy's turning to adultery can be explained: "the tenacity with which Loman clings to the punitive value of the system, his capacity for constantly obeying, reduce the dramatic space in which defiance can be expressed" (p. 225).
13. Cf. McMahon, 1972, pp. 42–45; Brater, 1982, pp. 115–126 and esp. 118–122.

STEVEN R. CENTOLA

Family Values in Death of a Salesman

Studies of Arthur Miller's *Death of a Salesman* invariably discuss Willy
Loman's self-delusion and moral confusion in relation to Miller's indictment
of the competitive, capitalistic society that is responsible for dehumanizing
the individual and transforming the once promising agrarian American
dream into an urban nightmare.[1] While Miller clearly uses Willy's collapse
to attack the false values of a venal American society, the play ultimately
captures the audience's attention not because of its blistering attack on social
injustice but because of its powerful portrayal of a timeless human dilemma.
Simply put, Miller's play tells the story of a man who, on the verge of death,
wants desperately to justify his life. As he struggles to fit the jagged pieces of
his broken life together, Willy Loman discovers that to assuage his guilt, he
must face the consequences of past choices and question the values inherent
in the life he has constructed for himself and his family. Willy's painful
struggle "to evaluate himself justly"[2] is finally what grips the play's audiences
around the world, for everyone, not just people who are culturally or
ideologically predisposed to embrace the American dream, can understand
the anguish that derives from "being torn away from our chosen image of
what and who we are in this world" ("Tragedy" 5).

One can appreciate the intensity of Willy's struggle only after isolating
the things that Willy values and after understanding how the complex

From *CLA Journal* 37, no. 1 (September 1993): 29-41. © 1993 by the College Language
Association.

interrelationship of opposed loyalties and ideals in Willy's mind motivates every facet of his speech and behavior in the play. By identifying and analyzing Willy Loman's values, we can uncover the intrinsic nature of Willy and Biff's conflict. Discussion of Willy's values specifically clarifies questions pertaining to Willy's infidelity and singular effort both to seek and escape from conscious recognition of the role he played in Biff's failure. Moreover, discussion of Willy's values helps us understand why Willy feels compelled to commit suicide. Ultimately, an analysis of Willy's values even helps to explain why *Death of a Salesman* is a tragedy, for in Willy Loman's drama of frustration, anguish, and alienation, we see a human struggle that is rooted in metaphysical as well as social and psychological concerns.

Throughout the play, Willy exhibits several important personality traits. Thoroughly convinced that "the man who makes an appearance in the business world, the man who creates personal interest, is the man who gets ahead,"[3] Willy is ever conscious of his appearance before others. Quite literally, Willy is probably obsessed with personal appearance because, in his mind, he was convinced himself that since he is destined for success, he must constantly dress the part. However, such fastidiousness also betrays his insecurity, something which often surfaces in his contradictory statements and emotional outbursts—these, of course, being a constant embarrassment for his family as well as a painful reminder to Willy of his ridiculous appearance before others. Beneath the surface optimism, therefore, lurk his frustration and keen sense of failure. That is why he can be spry, amusing, and cheerful one moment and then suddenly become quarrelsome, insulting, and sullen the next. Through Willy's incongruous behavior, Miller makes us sharply aware of the subterranean tensions dividing Willy.

Perhaps just as important as this, though, is the realization that with all of his seemingly absurd antics, and with his humor, quick intelligence, and warmth, Willy becomes likable, if not well liked. Even if we disagree with his actions, we still understand his anguish, share his suffering, and even come to admire him for his relentless pursuit of his impossible dream. With Miller, we come to see Willy as "extraordinary in one sense at least—he is driven to commit what to him is a consummate act of love through which he can hand down his selfhood, his identity. Perversely, perhaps, this has a certain noble claim if only in his having totally believed, and dreamed himself to death."[4]

Willy's quirky speech rhythms, his spontaneous utterance of success-formula platitudes, and his incessant contradictions flesh out his character and reveal his complex and troubled state of mind. More importantly, though, the poverty of his language exposes the conflict in his values that gives rise to all of his troubles in the play. The disparity between the hollowness of Willy's words and the passion with which he utters them underscore the tremendous variance between his deep feelings about and inadequate understanding of fatherhood, salesmanship, and success in one's personal life as well as in the business world in American society. For example, when Willy recites one of his stock phrases—such as "personality always wins the day" (*Salesman* 151)—he is expressing a long-held belief that has taken on the sanctity of a religious doctrine for him. The source of such success formulas may very well be books by Dale Carnegie and Russell Conwell—writers who popularized myths of the self-made man in the early twentieth century.[5] But without attributing such views to any particular influence, we can see that, in Willy's mind, such maxims are weighted with great authority; to him they represent nothing short of magical formulas for instant success. Like so many others in his society, he fails to see the banality in such clichés and is actually using bromidic language to bolster his own faltering self-confidence. By passionately repeating hackneyed phrases, Willy simultaneously tries to assure himself that he has made the right choices and has not wasted his life while he also prevents himself from questioning his conduct and its effect on his relations with others. Ironically, though, his speech says much more to anyone carefully listening.

Without knowing it, Willy cries out for help and denounces the life-lie that has destroyed his family. Even while yearning for success, Willy wants more than material prosperity; he wants to retrieve the love and respect of his family and the self-esteem which he has lost. Yet he goes about striving to achieve these goals in the wrong way because he has deceived himself into thinking that the values of the family he cherishes are inextricably linked with the values of the business world in which he works. He confuses the two and futilely tries to transfer one value system to the other's domain, creating nothing but chaos for himself and pain or embarrassment for everyone around him.

Willy's confusion has much to do with his own feelings of inadequacy as a father. His stubborn denial of these feelings, coupled with his misguided effort to measure his self-worth by the expression of love he thinks he can purchase in his family, only serves to aggravate his condition. Willy unwittingly hastens his own destruction by clinging fiercely to values that perpetually enforce his withdrawal from reality.

This problem is particularly evident in the way Willy approaches the profession of salesmanship. Instead of approaching his profession in the manner of one who understands the demands of the business world, Willy instead convinces himself that his success or failure in business has significance only in that it affects others'—particularly his family's—perception of him. He does not seek wealth for any value it has in itself;

financial prosperity is simply the visible sign that he is a good provider for his family.

The confluence of the personal and the professional in Willy's mind is evident as Willy tells Howard Wagner about a time when a salesman could earn a living and appreciate the importance of "respect," "comradeship," "gratitude," "friendship," and "personality" (*Salesman* 180–81)—terms that are repeatedly used by various members of the Loman family. Also significant is the fact that when explaining to his boss how he was introduced to the career of salesmanship, Willy does not use his brother's language or refer to the kinds of survival techniques which Ben undoubtedly would have employed to make his fortune in the jungle. Willy's speech to Howard suggests that Willy chooses to be a salesman because he wants to sell himself, more than any specific product, to others—a point underscored by the obvious omission in the play of any reference to the specific products that Willy carries around in his valises.

The value that Willy attaches to his role as a father is evident throughout the play in numerous passages that reveal his obsession with this image. Soon after the play begins, Willy's concern over his duty to "accomplish something" (*Salesman* 133) is evident. Thinking about the many years which he has spent driving from New York City to New England to sell his products, Willy ruefully wonders why he has worked "a lifetime to pay off [his] house ... and there's nobody to live in it" (*Salesman* 133). Obviously, Willy feels as though he has invested all of his life in his family and is not getting the kind of return he always expected. This feeling of futility makes him wonder whether he has failed as a father and impels him to explore his past—a psychological journey made effective theatrically by Miller's expressionistic use of lighting, music, and violation of wall-line boundaries. In almost every scene from his past, Willy's dialogue either comments on his role in his sons' development or shows his need to win Ben's approval of how he is rearing Biff and Happy. In scenes where he is congratulating Biff on his initiative for borrowing a regulation football to practice with (*Salesman* 144), or encouraging the boys to steal sand from the apartment house so that he can rebuild the front stoop (*Salesman* 158), or advising his sons to be well liked and make a good appearance in order to get ahead in the world (*Salesman* 146), Willy is unknowingly instilling values in his sons that will have a definite impact on their future development. He also does the same when he counsels Biff to "watch [his] schooling" (*Salesman* 142), tells his sons "Never leave a job till you're finished" (*Salesman* 143), or sentimentally praises America as "full of beautiful towns and fine, upstanding people" (*Salesman* 145). Even in scenes where he is troubled by Biff's stealing, failure of math, and renunciation of his love and authority after discovering his infidelity in Boston, Willy is probing only that part of his past that in some way calls into question his effectiveness as a father.

A look at the memory scenes also helps to explain why Willy values his family more than anything else in his life. Abandoned at an early age by his father, Willy has tried all his life to compensate for this painful loss. When Willy also suffers the sudden disappearance of his older brother, he nearly completely loses his self-confidence and a sense of his own identity as a male. His insecurity about his identity and role as a father is evident in the memory scene where he confesses to Ben that he feels "kind of temporary" (*Salesman* 159) about himself and seeks his brother's assurance that he is doing a good job of bringing up his sons:

> WILLY: Ben, my boys—can't we talk? They'd go into the jaws of hell for me, see, but I—
> BEN: William, you're being first-rate with your boys. Outstanding, manly chaps!
> WILLY, *hanging on to his words*: Oh, Ben, that's good to hear! Because sometimes I'm afraid that I'm not teaching them the right kind of—Ben, how should I teach them? (*Salesman* 159)

However, although Willy idolizes Ben and treasures his advice and opinions, Willy rarely does what Ben suggests and never imitates his pattern of behavior. In fact, until the end of Act II, when Ben appears entirely as a figment of Willy's imagination in a scene that has nothing to do with any remembered episode from his past, Willy implicitly rejects Ben's lifestyle and approach to business. There can be no doubt that in Willy's mind Ben's image stands for "success incarnate" (*Salesman* 152). Likewise, enshrined in Willy's memory, Ben's cryptic words magically ring "*with a certain vicious audacity*: William, when I walked into the jungle, I was seventeen. When I walked out I was twenty-one. And, by God, I was rich!" (*Salesman* 160). And there is always the tone of remorse in Willy's voice whenever he mentions Ben, for he associates his brother with his own missed opportunity: the Alaska deal which Willy turns down and with it the chance to make a fortune.

Clearly, then, Ben embodies more than just the image of success in Willy's mind; he also represents the road not taken. In other words, he is, in many ways, Willy's alter ego. Ben is the other self which Willy could have become had he chosen to live by a different code of ethics. Therefore, his presence in Willy's mind gives us insight into Willy's character by letting us see not only what Willy values but also what kinds of choices he has made in his life as a result of those values. For while Ben is undoubtedly the embodiment of one kind of American dream to Willy, so too is Dave

Singleman representative of another kind—and that is part of Willy's confusion: both men symbolize the American dream, yet in his mind they represent value systems that are diametrically opposed to each other. The memory scenes are important in bringing out this contrast and showing what Willy's perception of Ben reflects about Willy's own conflicting values.

In every memory scene in which Ben appears, his viewpoint is always contrasted with the perspective of another character. This counterbalancing occurs because, while Ben has had a significant impact on Willy's past that continues to remain alive in the present in his imagination, Ben's influence on Willy has actually been no stronger than that which has been exerted upon him by people like Linda and Dave Singleman—the latter actually having the strongest effect, possibly because he exists in Willy's mind only as an idealized image.

The characters' contrasting views, in essence, externalize warring factions within Willy's fractured psyche. Each character represents a different aspect of Willy's personality: Linda most often takes the part of his conscience; Charley generally expresses the voice of reason; and Ben seems to personify Willy's drive toward self-assertion and personal fulfillment. These forces compete against each other, struggling for dominance, but although one might temporarily gain an advantage over the others, no one maintains control indefinitely. All remain active in Willy, leaving him divided, disturbed, and confused.

Linda and Charley are the most conspicuous contrasts to Ben in the memory scenes. They represent that side of Willy that has deliberately chosen not to follow in his brother's footsteps. Yet their views are not remembered as being superior to Ben's, for the image of Ben remains shrouded in mystery and splendor in Willy's memory and serves as a reminder not only of lost opportunity but also of the possibility of transforming dreams into reality. Ben's apparition haunts Willy and prods him to question his choices in life. However, since Willy both wants answers and dreads finding them, tension, not resolution, prevails in these scenes.

Such tension is evident, for example, in the scene where Charley and Ben disagree over Willy's handling of the boys' stealing:

CHARLEY: Listen, if they steal any more from that building the watchman'll put the cops on them!
LINDA, *to Willy*: Don't let Biff ...
  Ben laughs lustily.
WILLY: You shoulda seen the lumber they brought home last week. At least a dozen six-by-tens worth all kinds a money.
CHARLEY: Listen, if that watchman—

WILLY: I gave them hell, understand. But I got a couple of fearless characters there.

CHARLEY: Willy, the jails are full of fearless characters.

BEN, *clapping Willy on the back, with a laugh at Charley*: And the stock exchange, friend! (*Salesman* 158)

Tension is also clearly present when Ben suddenly trips Biff while they are sparring and consequently receives a cold, disapproving stare from Linda (*Salesman* 158). Linda's opposition is even more apparent as she diminishes Ben's influence over Willy during their conversation about the Alaska deal; by reminding Willy of the successful Dave Singleman, she rekindles within him his love of the profession that he associates with family values and the unlimited possibilities inherent within the American dream (*Salesman* 183–84). Ironically, Linda could actually be said to have hurt Willy by upholding his illusions. Nevertheless, she is instrumental in helping him reject Ben's business ethics, even though Willy does not recognize the value inherent in his choice and foolishly torments himself only with the memory of missed opportunity.

Unlike Willy, Ben functions comfortably in the modern business world. His life history provides confirmation of Howard Wagner's pronouncement that "business is business" (*Salesman* 180), and like Charley, he is a realist who has no illusions about what it takes to be a success. He is a survivor who undoubtedly made a fortune in the jungle through the kinds of ruthless acts which he performs in his sparring session with Biff. He suggests as much when he warns Biff: "Never fight fair with a stranger, boy. You'll never get out of the jungle that way" (*Salesman* 158). Ben's drive for self-fulfillment is undoubtedly predicated upon his denial of any responsibility for others and his repudiation of the values which Willy cherishes and associates with his romanticized view of family life and the past.

In dramatic contrast to the image of this ruthless capitalist stands the idealized figure of Dave Singleman. In Willy's mind, the image of Dave Singleman reflects Willy's unfaltering conviction that personal salvation can be linked with success, that business transactions can be made by people who respect and admire each other. Willy practically worships this legendary salesman who, at the age of eighty-four, "drummed merchandise in thirty-one states" by picking up a phone in his hotel room and calling buyers who remembered and loved him (*Salesman* 180). The legend of Dave Singleman so strongly impresses Willy that he decides that success results from "who you know and the smile on your face! It's contacts ... being liked" (*Salesman* 184) that guarantee a profitable business. Willy clings to the illusion that he can become another Dave Singleman—in itself an impossible task since no one can become another person, a fact underscored by the name *Single*man, which obviously calls attention to the individual's uniqueness—even though Willy knows he lives in an era when business is "all cut and dried, and there's no chance for bringing friendship to bear—or personality" (*Salesman* 180–81). He fails to see the folly of his dream and ends up passing on not only his dream but also his confusion to Biff and Happy.

Their dilemma not only mirrors Willy's identity crisis but also indicts him for his ineptitude as a father. Moreover, seeing his failure reflected in the lives of his sons further intensifies Willy's guilt and hastens his decline.

Both sons are "*lost*" and "*confused*" (*Salesman* 136). They have inherited their father's powerful dreams but have no true understanding of how to attain them. Biff is more troubled than Happy because he is more conscious of this problem. Biff knows that he does not belong in the business world but still feels obligated to build his future there since that is what his father expects of him. He would prefer to work on a farm, performing manual labor, but he has learned from Willy not to respect such work. In Willy's mind, physical labor is tainted with the suggestion of something demeaning. When Biff suggests that they work as carpenters, Willy reproachfully shouts: "Even your grandfather was better than a carpenter.... Go back to the West! Be a carpenter, a cowboy, enjoy yourself!" (*Salesman* 166). With gibes like this in mind, Biff never feels completely satisfied working as a farmhand and tortures himself with guilt over his failure to satisfy Willy's demand that he do something extraordinary with his life.

In the harrowing climactic scene, however, Biff puts an end to his self-deception and tries to force his family to face the truth about him and themselves. He shatters the illusion of his magnificence by firmly telling Willy: "I'm not bringing home any prizes any more, and you're going to stop waiting for me to bring them home!" (*Salesman* 217). Knowing that his days of glory are past and that his dreams have nothing to do with Willy's vision of success for him, Biff embraces his life and stops living a lie. At the play's end, Biff confidently asserts: "I know who I am ..." (*Salesman* 222). However, while he manages to succeed in his own quest for certitude, he fails to prevent Willy's self-destruction.

Willy commits suicide because he "cannot settle for half but must pursue his dream of himself to the end."[6] He convinces himself that only his death can restore his prominence in his family's eyes and retrieve for him his lost sense of honor. Perhaps without ever being fully conscious of his motives, Willy feels that his sacrifice will purge him of his guilt and make him worthy of Biff's love. When he realizes that he never lost Biff's love, Willy decides that he must die immediately so that he can preserve that love and not jeopardize it with further altercations. In his desperation to perform one extraordinary feat for his son so that he can once and for all verify his greatness and confirm his chosen image of himself in Biff's eyes, Willy turns to what he knows best: selling. He literally fixes a cash value on his life and, in killing himself, tries to complete his biggest sale. Willy thinks that by bequeathing Biff twenty thousand dollars, he will provide conclusive proof of his immutable essence as a good father, a goal that has obsessed him ever since the day Biff discovered Willy's infidelity in Boston.

When Biff finds Willy with Miss Francis, Biff is horrified to see the face behind the mask that Willy wears. This sudden revelation of the naked soul in all its weakness and imperfection is more than Biff can bear because he has been trained to elude reality and substitute lies for truth. Beneath Biff's scornful gaze, Willy becomes nothing more than a "liar," a "phony little fake" (*Salesman* 208). Such condemnation leaves Willy feeling disgraced and alienated, so he retreats into the sanctuary of the past in a frantic effort to recapture there what is irretrievably lost in the present: his innocence and chosen identity. He opts for self-deception as a way of maintaining his distorted image of himself—a costly decision that eventually causes his psychological disorientation and death. He goes to his grave, as Biff puts it, without ever knowing "who he was" (*Salesman* 221).

However, Biff is only partially right when he says: Willy "had the wrong dreams. All, all, wrong ..." (*Salesman* 221). Willy does deny a valuable part of his existence—his aptitude for manual labor—and spends most of his life mistakenly believing that values associated with the family open the door to success in the business world. He also transfers his confusion to his sons. Yet, in spite of his failings, Willy must ultimately be appreciated for valuing so highly the family and his role as a father. Even though he has misconceptions about this role, his inspiring pursuit of his forever elusive identity as the perfect father makes him a tragic figure. That is why Miller writes: "There is a nobility ... in Willy's struggle. Maybe it comes from his refusal ever to relent, to give up" (*Beijing* 27). Against all odds, Willy Loman demands that his life have "meaning and significance and honor" (*Beijing* 49).

Of course, in many ways, Willy ultimately fails to fulfill his dream. The Requiem clearly shows that he is not immortalized in death. His funeral is certainly not like the grand one he had imagined, and he still remains misunderstood by his family. But death does not defeat Willy Loman. The Requiem proves that his memory will continue to live on in those who truly mattered to him while he was alive. He might not have won their respect, but he is definitely loved—and perhaps that is all that Willy ever really hoped to achieve. Miller says that what Willy wanted "was to excel, to win out over anonymity and meaninglessness, to love and be loved, and above all, perhaps, to *count*."[7] After considering the importance of family values to Willy Loman, we are decidedly more inclined to say that he does, indeed, *count*— and we can perhaps better understand why his struggle and death make Miller's drama a tragedy of lasting and universal significance.

NOTES

1. See, for example, Henry Popkin, "Arthur Miller: The Strange Encounter," *Sewanee Review* 68 (Winter 1960): 48–54; Barry Edward Gross, "Peddler and Pioneer in *Death of a Salesman*," *Modern Drama* 7 (February 1965): 405–10; Thomas E. Porter, *Myth and Modern American Drama* (Detroit: Wayne State UP, 1969) 127–52; Ronald Hayman, *Arthur Miller* (New York: Frederick Ungar, 1972); Christopher Bigsby, *A Critical Introduction to Twentieth-Century American Drama* (Cambridge: Cambridge UP, 1984) II, 135–248; and Kay Stanton, "Women and the American Dream of *Death of a Salesman*," *Feminist Rereadings of Modern American Drama*, ed. June Schlueter (Madison: Fairleigh Dickinson UP, 1989) 67–102.

2. Arthur Miller, "Tragedy and the Common Man," *The Theater Essays of Arthur Miller*, ed. Robert A. Martin (New York: Penguin Books, 1978) 4. Hereafter cited parenthetically in the text as "Tragedy."

3. Arthur Miller, *Death of a Salesman, Arthur Miller's Collected Plays* (New York: Viking, 1957) I. 146. Hereafter cited parenthetically in the text as *Salesman*.

4. Arthur Miller, *Salesman in Beijing* (New York: Viking, 1984) 190. Hereafter cited parenthetically in the text as *Beijing*.

5. See Dale Carnegie, *How to Win Friends and Influence People* (New York: Simon and Schuster, 1936); and Russell H. Conwell, *Acres of Diamonds* (New York: Harper, 1905). Discussion of these texts and other works which popularized the success myth can he found in Porter, pp. 127–52.

6. Arthur Miller, Introd., *Arthur Miller's Collected Plays* I, 34.

7. Arthur Miller, *Timebends: A Life* (New York: Grove, 1987) 184.

STEPHEN BARKER

The Crisis of Authenticity:
Death of a Salesman *and the Tragic Muse*

> In *Death of a Salesman*, Miller has formulated a statement about the
> nature of human crises in the twentieth century which seems,
> increasingly, to be applicable to the entire fabric of civilized experience.
> —Esther Merle Jackson

Even those who have disputed the right of *Death of a Salesman* to claim the
stature of modern tragedy have been highly aware of its dialogue with that
enigmatic and elevated genre. Ironically, Miller's defense of the play as
modern tragedy only serves to conceal, within its humanistic fervor, many
good reasons for treating the play as tragic. Other critical approaches to the
play also conceal, inadvertently, tragic treatments of it. In fact, the standard
generic battle over the play produces numerous puzzles and opportunities
for interpretive response. To consider the play within the context of
traditional notions of the tragic, notions that date back to Plato, is to invite
an altered tragic vision. As mimesis of cultural crisis, *Death of a Salesman* must
be treated as an exemplum of the tragic vision in the twentieth century,
quintessentially defining the crisis of authenticity that is the tragic.

In this essay I consider the context, pretext, and text of *Death of a
Salesman* as tragic crisis itself.

From *Approaches to Teaching Miller's Death of a Salesman*, edited by Matthew C. Roudané. © 1995
by the Modern Language Association of America.

CONTEXT

Crisis

> The tragic vision, a product of crisis and of shock, is an
> expression of man only in an extreme situation, never in a normal
> or routine one.... a distillate of the rebellion, the godlessness
> which, once induced by crisis, purifies itself by rejecting all
> palliatives. (Krieger 20)

Tragedy, tragic vision, and the Tragic Muse are normative cultural
identifiers.[1] They are a collective reminder of what we were and what we
imagine we want to become; from its inception in the *tragosodos*, the "goat
songs" whose dithyrambic intensity galvanized early Greek audiences of
tragedy, the tragic has served this self-reflexive purpose. As a result of its role
as cultural identifier, the tragic idea defines itself as a function of that crisis to
which Murray Krieger refers. Krieger's crisis-context, articulated in *The
Tragic Vision*, for both tragedy (a literary work) and the tragic vision (its
cultural context) rely on two misunderstood Greek words, *katharsis* and
mimesis.[2] *Katharsis*, mentioned only once (vaguely) by Aristotle in the *Poetics*
(1449b), means "purity" or "purgation" but is widely interpretable depending
on one's view of purity or purgation. Aristotle is impossibly vague on this
subject; *katharsis* becomes, as a result, a diachronic, culturally determined
concept bracketed within the tragic vision. *Mimesis*, which we have come to
understand as "imitation," obscuring Aristotle's practicality, should be
thought of, rather, as "illusion" or "pretense" (see Kaufmann 33–41).

How different is Aristotle's definition of tragedy when it appears this
way: "[A] tragedy, then, is the illusion of an action that is serious and also, as
having magnitude, complete in itself" (1449b), or "[T]ragedy is essentially an
illusion not of persons but of action and life" (1450a). Tragedy, in this revised
view, is not the agent and result of the correspondence of planes of existence
but a sign of their disintegration—not the representation of an external
"reality" but the transmutation of external reification into performative
illusion. As Miller points out, "[T]he Greeks could probe the very heavenly
origin of their ways and return to confirm the rightness of laws, and Job
could face God in anger, demanding his right, and end in submission. But for
a moment everything is in suspension, nothing is accepted." All culture is
threatened, and in the moment of this crisis, "this stretching and tearing
apart of the cosmos," the tragic vision is born. What is "in suspension," for
Miller as for the Greeks, is man's ability rightly and fully to "secure his
rightful place in the world," to lay claim to "his whole due as a personality,"

through "the indestructible will of man to achieve his humanity" ("Tragedy," *Salesman: Text* 146). For Miller, the tragic vision provides man and humanity with the tear through which to glimpse him and itself.[3] The tragic vision thus presents "a crisis and a shock," "an expression of man only in an extreme situation." Willy, at his first entrance, is disoriented and frightened, in crisis, indeed at a critical crossroads in his life: unable to travel but defined by traveling, this man must redefine himself and thus everyone around him. Miller's response to this crisis—including its self-delusions and rebellions against constraints in which, "rejecting all palliatives," Willy gropes through his downfall—depicts the illusion of Willy's psychic crisis and suggests our own individuated one in contemporary culture. Indeed, this critical introspection occupied Miller from his conception of the play, whose original title, *The Inside of His Head*, came from Miller's original idea of a huge human head that, suspended above the stage, would literally open up; the play was to depict the "experience of disintegration" (R. Williams, *Modern Tragedy* 12) in Willy but as experienced by the viewer or reader.

Authenticity

Death of a Salesman portrays the crisis of contemporary culture; culture, in turn, is the perpetual crisis of authenticity, according to Freud's use of the term (*kultur*) in *Civilization and Its Discontents*, in which civilization's purpose "is to combine single human individuals, and after that families, then races, peoples and nations, into one great unity, the unity of mankind" (69) for reasons of safety, control, and "order." Cultural identity is the rooted goal of civilized man. Even though it must be remembered that in general (and specifically in terms of Willy, Linda, and their sons) this goal is contrary to the raw individuality and aggression of "human nature," it is still the goal of Homo sapiens.[4] This critical struggle for authenticity occurs within the context of the tragic vision:

> The tragic visionary may at the crucial moment search within and find himself "hollow at the core," because he has been seized from without by the hollowness of his moral universe, whose structure and meaning have until then sustained him. What the shock reveals to its victim—the existential absurdity of the moral life—explodes the meaning of the moral life, its immanent god and ground. (Krieger 15)

This absurdity, which is not meaningless but, on the contrary, fraught with meaning, explodes the myth of the moral life precisely because it will not fit obediently into a synchronically operable view of "immanent god and ground." Within this context of tragic self-revelation Willy (qua salesman) strives to experience himself as somehow authentic. Throughout our tradition this quest has been an urgent concern and has formed our idea of the tragic.

A further complication of Aristotelian tragic authentication as Miller uses it in *Death of a Salesman* is its reliance on a certain jargon. An appropriate reference in the investigation of this issue is Theodor Adorno's critique of Heideggerian existentialism, *The Jargon of Authenticity*, which explores ways in which "false" rhetoric (tautology) produces an "ideological mystification" of human experience that "bars the message from the experience which is to ensoul it" (6). The aptness of this jargon of authenticity to *Death of a Salesman* is clear: Willy becomes a function of the "high spiritual language" of the capitalist ethic, with its camaraderie and alienation; his involvement with Dave Singleman and with Ben are nothing less than spiritual; what is most unauthentic is taken for the grounding of life. Biff, Happy, and Linda all buy into this jargon in their own ways. Adorno's critique of the jargon of authenticity declares that it distances one from the "aura" of the authentic to which the words point but which they do not and cannot "capture"—and which is in fact undermined by its own nature. The nomenclature of America's "religion of success" shows itself as what Adorno calls "words that are sacred without sacred content, as frozen emanations; the terms of the jargon of authenticity are products of the disintegration of the aura" (9–10). For example, Willy Loman's repeated reference to being "well-liked" and statements such as "in those days there was personality in it.... There was respect, and comradeship, and gratitude in it" (81) manifest this dangerous jargon. As Adorno writes,

> [T]he nimbus in which the words are being wrapped, like oranges in tissue paper, takes under its own direction the mythology of language, as if the radiant force of the words could not yet quite be trusted.... The jargon becomes practicable along the whole scale, reaching from sermon to advertisement. In the medium of the concept the jargon becomes surprisingly similar to the habitual practices of advertising. (43)

In just this way, Adorno suggests, Willy's jargon of self-authenticity, which is purportedly a language for life, becomes one for death.

One of Adorno's central ideas, linking him closely to Nietzsche's tragic mode, is the challenge to "real experience" that the dialectic with authenticity enforces: "The bourgeois form of rationality has always needed irrational supplements, in order to maintain itself as what it is, continuing injustice through justice. Such *irrationality in the midst of the rational* is the working atmosphere of authenticity" (47; emphasis mine). These remarks echo Nietzsche's on the Dionysian and Apollonian in *The Birth of Tragedy* and on cruelty in *The Will to Power*. They play a central part in Willy's sense of injustice and his fearful indignation. Tragic authentication can never be trusted, since it is always a function of authenticating jargon.

Identity

Tragic authenticity and its perpetual crisis stage themselves, as is increasingly clear, as a crisis of identity. When we ask what authentication authenticates, we (and Miller) must answer "the self." This imperative, however, is self-evidently another tautology of rhetoric, as Adorno—echoing Nietzsche—shows:

> Authenticity, in the traditional language of philosophy, would be identical with subjectivity as such. But in that way, unnoticed, subjectivity also becomes the judge of authenticity. Since it is denied any objective determination, authenticity is determined by the arbitrariness of the subject, which is authentic to itself. (126)

Our great hope, like Willy's, is that we will be "identical with subjectivity as such"; this "identity thinking" (Adorno 139) consumes Willy, who is naively caught in what Nietzsche calls "imaginative" lying (*Human* 54). This perpetual crisis of identity has been evolving at least since the Enlightenment and continued to do so even after Hegel's undermining of the noble tragic hero and his relation to moira, a notion necessary to Miller's claims about tragedy and the common man. Krieger's tragic vision asserts, indeed, that since Hegel's turn toward introspection (which is still bound up in the divine as pure knowledge), the conditions for the tragic have shifted and are no longer determined by Hegelian universality justly imposing itself on the tragic individual; now, Krieger says, the tragic figure stands "outside the universal," solipsistically isolated in a world where justice has passed from the universal to the individual whose rebellion is often inadvertent or unconscious—from Büchner's Woyzeck to Willy Loman. In the latter we confront a tragic "hero" who not only lacks heroism but desires to merge with and be a part of a social landscape that cannot or will not accept him.[5] The home Willy has built ("he was so wonderful with his hands" [138]) is purportedly the symbol of that resting place among the "vastness of strangers" (Miller, "Family" 233) that the solipsistic individual seeks; but Willy's hands are useless to build the home he desires, defined by Miller as "the everlastingly sought balance between order and the need of our souls for freedom" (233), which is a condition, not a place.

Willy carries his tragic homelessness around with him wherever he goes, since it is something by which he knows himself. This homelessness of self-division is what finally makes *Salesman* the tragedy of the common man. Willy is the exemplar of (American capitalist) society, attempting to achieve his humanity and his identity in the face of numerous tragic sunderings. Willy's typicality is explored provocatively by Raymond Williams in *Modern Tragedy*, in which Williams supports the view that Willy is neither a rebel nor a nonconformist but, rather, a frustrated conformist to Nietzsche's lie of culture: "Willy Loman is a man who from selling things has passed to selling himself, and has become, in effect, a commodity which like other commodities will at a certain point be discarded by the laws of the economy. He brings tragedy down on himself, not by opposing the lie, but by living it" (104). Miller corroborates Williams's view of the "laws of the economy" as they affect Willy, as though Willy's condition is quantifiable on a social ledger: *Salesman*, he writes, "was meant to be less a play than a fact; it refused admission to its author's opinions and opened itself to a revelation of process and the operations of an ethic, of social laws of action no less powerful in their effects upon individuals than any tribal law administered by gods with names" (Introduction 27).

An inevitable result of the contemporary tragic vision's anomie is its sense of the failure and falling off of culture. The cancellation of "old truths" in *Death of a Salesman* has had this effect; anomie and alienation occur in the context of the memory of a previous, better state of things, real or imagined. Miller sees all tragedy as deriving from this sense of loss, as showing "man's deprivation of a once-extant state of bliss unjustly shattered—a bliss, a state of equilibrium, which the hero (and his audience) is attempting to reconstruct or to recreate with new, latter-day life materials." It is as though we "once had an identity, a *being*, somewhere in the past, which in the present has lost its completeness, its definiteness" ("Family" 223). In Willy's effort at reconstruction, his hands are not in fact so wonderful. The tragic vision entails a fear of cultural enervation. Miller's tragic sense here has an interesting correlative in William Faulkner's. Combining the social and the personal, both Miller and Faulkner demonstrate an ambivalence concerning inner and outer realities; in this ambivalence the American dream is portrayed. The complex admixture of inner and outer states orchestrated in the great vortex of *As I Lay Dying*, with its downward spiral toward Jefferson and the replacement of Darl's narrative voice by the inarticulate Jewel (after Darl is committed to an asylum at the end) is a tremendously tragic diminution, the dying off of culture. Tragedy has fulfilled this role since before the earliest Dionysian festivals, as Nietzsche asserts: the cultural crisis portrayed by tragedy is always a fear of (cultural) death, which is the death of the self. Willy Loman tries in death to reaffirm his lost identity and his lost will, as Miller declares: "the lasting appeal of tragedy is due to our need to face the fact of death in order to strengthen ourselves for life" (Introduction 27). Tragedy, as reaffirmed by Miller, is truly a life-or-death crisis.

PRETEXT: THE CONTEMPORARY AMERICAN TRAGEDY

I identify myself in Language, but only by losing myself in it like an object. (Lacan 63)

I use the word *pretext* here in two ways: first, in its sense of falseness or deception; second, in the sense by which we are here opening a wide circle of texts before closing and in order to close in on a single text. Both senses exude a trace of *praetexere*, "to weave before," to pretend. In this sense, *pretext* carries the same burden as does *mimesis*, according to Walter Kaufmann's analysis of the latter as pretense (see appendix I). To suggest that *Death of a Salesman* is a play about the interweavings of pretense, that the American tragic dream is one of illusion unfulfilled, would be to claim the obvious. But Miller takes the critique of American illusion a step farther: for Willy, "the [tragic] motif is the growth of illusion until it destroys the individual and leaves the children to whom he transmitted it incapable of dealing with reality" (Schumach 6). "On the play's opening night," Miller recounts in *Timebends*, "a woman who shall not be named was outraged, calling it 'a time bomb under American capitalism'; I hoped it was, or at least under the bullshit of capitalism, this pseudo life that thought to touch the clouds by standing on top of a refrigerator, waving a paid-up mortgage at the moon, victorious at last" (184).

In illusion, Miller attacks illusion; but here I want to recontextualize, using a patently Lacanian image by which to present the illusory self against which our illusions echo: "The American Dream is a largely unacknowledged screen in front of which all American writing plays itself out—the screen of the perfectibility of man. Whoever is writing in the United States is using the American Dream as an ironical pole of his story. It's a failure *in relation* to that screen" (Roudané, *Conversations* 362). Evoking the shade of Lacan's impossible dialectical self, the *je* that can never be uttered, Miller introduces the reader to the project of contemporary tragedy—without whose critical urgency, Miller says, "a genuine onslaught upon the veils that cloak the present" ("Family" 233) would be impossible.

In fact, the crisis of the American illusion is rhetorical, as Lacan suggests. The law is a rhetorical superstructure of "success," self-serving and duplicitous (a constant pretext); Willy's hamartia is a transgression against this law. Miller shows that a "failure" in business and in society has no right to live; he conceived of the play as a "race" between the meting out of this sentence of death and the opposing system of love that Biff finally learns, too late to save Willy. But even this system of love is a structure of pretexts: Willy can feel nothing beyond the veil or screen of his constitutive fictions. Harold Clurman anticipates this falsehood in a review of the play:

> Salesmanship implies a certain element of fraud: the ability to put over or sell a commodity regardless of its intrinsic usefulness.... To place all value in the mechanical act of selling and in self-enrichment impoverishes the human beings who are rendered secondary to the deal. To possess himself fully, a man must have an intimate connection with that with which he deals as well as with the person with whom he deals. When the connection is no more than an exchange of commodities, the man ceases to be a man, becomes a commodity himself, a spiritual cipher. ("Nightlife" 49–50)

That Willy's "product" is never identified becomes even more interesting in the light of Clurman's comments: Willy is the cipher of an empty signifier. His jargon of authenticity actively prevents his reifying himself. As the author of his own tragedy, Willy is prevented from taking meaningful action by the narratives that identify him. These narratives are themselves active illusions (e.g., Ben's apocryphal life stories and the epos of Dave Singleman) that put Willy into the role of Krieger's tragic visionary, the "extremist" who "despite his intermingling with the stuff of experience ... finds himself transformed from character to parable" (20). Willy tries to learn the requisites of self-consciousness from Ben and Dave, but since they are themselves dialectical constructs within Willy's mind, and since Willy does not know this, he must fail. Willy misunderstands the ontological dilemma in which he is caught, a dilemma that has an ancient pedigree in the pretext of tragedy. Greek tragedy ends with choral closure, *Hamlet* with the perpetuation of the tragic story in Hamlet's charge to Horatio: the resolution of tragedy, structurally, is in its transformation into tragic narrative.

Willy's tragic error, his hamartia, failure to succeed, is in general that self-*méconnaissance* at the heart of the American illusion. Inherent in its rhetoric of transcendence is a crisis of transcription in which Willy is caught in his own crisis of self-vision, unable to clarify his attitude toward value and meaning, ambivalent about the nature of ethical action, and finally unable even to define the tragic; he does not see the tragedy of his own life. He searches perpetually through the "wordless darkness that underlies all verbal truth" (*Timebends* 144), not because that darkness has secrets which would finally ground him but because he fails to recognize the source of his own identity—his and his culture's constitutive tragic self-narratives. The disease of unrelatedness, whose symptoms are growing despair and a loss of meaning, is the ontological absence at the heart of ego-consciousness, ignored or transcended by the American illusion.

TEXT: THE CIVILIZING ACT

WILLY. I'm not interested in stories about the past or any crap of
that kind because the woods are burning, boys, you
understand? There's a big blaze going on all around. (107)

Death of a Salesman seems to want us to see Willy authenticated in Biff's embrace in the play's penultimate scene; in Miller's view, Willy goes to his death exalted in this authentication: he "has bestowed power on his posterity" (Introduction 27). But even Willy can see that the insurance policy for which he has sold himself is a fiction, a text founded on illusion. The myth of authenticity in which Willy believes is an aesthetic of absence: Willy's real insurance policy is the texture of stories with which he has fought for his authentication. Willy's suicide is an embracing of a last chimerical myth. The unbridgeable gulf between Willy's desire for authenticity, for "full human character," and his blindness in achieving it replicates the great Dionysian crisis at the epicenter of the tragic vision. Willy's mounting frenzy through the course of the play, culminating in the (mock-)Zarathustran heights of that penultimate scene, reminds us of Nietzsche's admonition at the beginning of Zarathustra's self-authentication story:

"Man is a rope, tied between beast and overman—a rope over
an abyss. A dangerous across, a dangerous on-the-way, a
dangerous looking-back, a dangerous shuddering and stopping.
"What is great in man is that he is a bridge and not an end:
what can be loved in man is that he is an *overture* and a *going
under*." (*Zarathustra* 4)[6]

Willy is stretched on that same abysmal rack, never an end but always a bridge, a traveling man, on the move, wandering through a life that at numerous levels acts as a mimesis of the fundamental dilemma of tragic *méconnaissance*; he does not and cannot recognize himself. This tragedy, according to Miller, is the crisis and the reality of American life.

The play's world, like Zarathustra's, is one not of characterological reality but of civilizing texts, from Willy's first travel story of his last, abortive New England trip, to Happy's story of how he is going to show everyone that Willy had a "good dream" (139).[7] Willy speaks to Ben before Ben enters and after Ben leaves (44, 52) because what matters most to Willy is not Ben but Ben's stories. Since Willy has never "solidified" (72), never understood his own sublimation into the epos from which he fabricates himself, he has not passed this self-analysis to his sons; thus Happy is the incarnation of Willy (both are cheats, philanderers, and princes), and Biff, whose "training" has been much more complex (as we discover in the surfacing of the ultimate repression, what I call the Standish Arms Epiphany, which is not so much a repressed experience as the repressed story of an experience), "can't take hold of some kind of life" (54) and so takes hold of the dark side of the commodity exchange ritual by becoming a thief. Since Willy's stories center on his and Biff's success, the story of Bill Oliver is a vital one; when Willy is at his nadir, in Stanley's restaurant after Biff has gone through the illusion-destroying facts about his relationship with Oliver, Willy simply responds that he has been fired and that now "[t]he gist of it is that I haven't got a story left in my head" (107). Deprived of stories, Willy is "just a guy," as Happy so brutally declares (115).

The crisis of authenticity in *Death of a Salesman*, a subset of the crisis of rhetorical power, can finally be unlocked with three keys: self-naming, figures of desire, and the compensation of art for the tragic vision.

Self-Naming

In *Timebends*, Miller describes Willy as a man "who could never cease trying, like Adam, to name himself" (182). But if the self, so-called, is a palimpsest of texts written over one another, and if the original inscription, the apocryphal true identity, is chimerical, then the self is a system of dysfunctional metaphors in which, while one is always trying to "make one's mark," that mark is always a sign of absence.[8] Nonetheless, self-naming is a vital part of the tragic misrecognition in *Death of a Salesman*. Willy has had to name himself because "well, Dad left when I was such a baby and I never had a chance to talk to him and I still feel—kind of temporary about myself" (51). Unable to inscribe himself solidly, Willy has (or believes he has) named

others: Biff, Happy, Howard ("I named him. I named him Howard" [97]).
Willy does not see, as Charley tells him, that naming "don't mean anything"
(97). If one's name is Salesman, what one sells names one; being unable to
sell means having no name. When Happy denies Willy's identity in Stanley's
bar, he thus speaks accurately: the now storyless Willy is not his father but
"just a guy"—in some respect not Hap's father at all. Willy is simply the
central figure in a convocation of characters whose need, greater than
"hunger, sex, or thirst," is "to leave a thumbprint somewhere on the world,"
to know "that one has carefully inscribed one's name on a cake of ice on a hot
July day" (Miller, Introduction 25). This urge toward self-naming accounts
for Biff's otherwise incomprehensible act of stealing Bill Oliver's pen: by
appropriating the signing tool, Biff tries to appropriate the ability to sign for
himself. He realizes immediately that this goal is impossible and even
embarrassing; he throws the pen away.

Figures of Desire

Miller gathers around the play a web of figures who exist only as subjects and
objects of desire. This "chorus" of characters takes Willy as its focus and acts
as a cultural medium. Seen in the light of this cultural medium, Willy's desire
to be "well-liked" takes on new significance. To be well liked is a challenge
to any salesman, but in the cultural medium every man is a salesman, every
woman a saleswoman, acting out the desire to sell a whole and complete self
to others, who will then judge the salesperson as substantial.[9] This cultural
web of emblematic characters and their stories of desire for self-
authentication range outward from Willy to his family to those in close
proximity to it (Charley, Bernard, Howard) to those at a greater distance
(Happy's boss, Stanley, people in Stanley's bar) to those who are pure
narrative (Willy's father, Ben, Dave Singleman). We have seen how Hap's
and Biff's stories center on a desire to be substantiated; Biff's "I know who
I am" (138) is as much a rhetorical dream as is Willy's. Linda, too, has
struggled for this solidification, fought Ben for Willy, won, and built a dream
of security. Linda's tragedy is that she has achieved everything she set out to
achieve yet can save neither the family nor Willy because she does not
understand the narrative nature of her life. Like Happy's boss, the
merchandise manager who cannot be satisfied with anything he has, the
concentric circles of characters emanating from Willy, the play's central well
of desire, reenact the crucial act of narratized desire.

Most interesting in this respect are the play's absent storytellers of
desire, the chorus of chimerical figures who frame Willy's self-search. These
characters—Dave Singleman, Willy's father, Ben—ground the central

narratives of the play and establish the perimeters of its tragic vision of rhetorical power. Each of these figures acts as a custodian of self-ratification. Dave Singleman is the model upon whom Willy bases his standards of success; we must work our way back through Dave Singleman to reach Willy's two deeper father figures. In fact, Dave Singleman is a palimpsestic story written over that of the "real" father:

> Oh, yeah, my father lived many years in Alaska. He was an adventurous man. We've got quite a streak of self-reliance in our family. I thought I'd go out with my older brother and try to locate him, and maybe settle in the North with the old man. And I was almost decided to go, when I met a salesman in the Parker House. His name was Dave Singleman. (81)

The famous story of the gentleman-salesman shows two things: Singleman's legend and Willy's failure to emulate his idol.[10] Willy's vital long speech to Howard concludes, "[T]hey don't know me any more" (81). As for the father as figure of desire, Willy evokes his ghost through Ben, precisely because he feels "kind of temporary" about himself. Willy invokes Ben to tell Biff and Hap the story of the father in an apotheosis of desire:

> WILLY. ... Please tell about Dad. I want my boys to hear. I want them to know the kind of stock they spring from. All I remember is a man with a big beard, and I was in Mamma's lap, sitting around a fire, and some kind of high music.
> BEN. His flute. He played his flute.
> WILLY. Sure, the flute, that's right!
> *New music is heard, a high, rollicking tune.*
> BEN. Father was a very great and a very wild-hearted man. We would start in Boston, and he'd toss the whole family into the wagon, and then he'd drive the team right across the country; through Ohio, and Indiana, Michigan, Illinois, and all the Western states. And we'd stop in the towns and sell the flutes that he'd made on the way. Great inventor, Father. With one gadget he made more in a week than a man like you could make in a lifetime.
> WILLY. That's just the way I'm bringing them up, Ben—rugged, well liked, all-around. (48–49)

The original inventor, the great man whose every idea was a gold mine and who was at the same time an Odyssean wanderer: this man is not Willy's father but a wonderfully and impossibly romanticized narrative of the Ur-father, the narrative behind Willy's self-crisis. Because he does not understand his own narratives, Willy cannot dissociate himself from the impossible romanticism the story of the father establishes. Like Miller's flute music, which implicates the reader-audience in the dream of the father, that paternal epos operates as a pervasive index of desire.

By the same token, the teller of that story (Ben) is himself a kind of father-narrator whose stories have a more direct impact on Willy's tragic dilemma than Willy's actual father does. Ben, not the father, receives Willy's accolade as "the only man I ever met who knew all the answers" (45). Ben knows all the answers because he has a story (of success) for all occasions: his story anticipates all Willy's inadequacies and desires for himself. Ben's triumph is not just that he went into the jungle and came out rich but that in the jungle Ben became solid, substantial. Ben has reified himself and solidified his story (he always tells the same one) in a way that Willy never could. Willy never understands, though Linda does, that Ben's threat is precisely this solidification: Ben and his story represent the breakup of the family, success at the price of humanness. Ben, like Faulkner's magical bear of the same name, is pure story divorced from life, and indeed when Willy is able to tell his own story in the same solid way, he is at the threshold of death. It is Ben who counsels Willy to kill himself for Biff's "inheritance." This insane advice, which completely ignores both Biff and Willy and manifests itself as a heap of platitudes ("it does take a great kind of a man to crack the jungle" [133]) is the aberrant vision of Willy's desire—and its tragic formulation. The "diamonds in the jungle" Ben seems to offer Willy are the chimerical authentication Willy cannot achieve.

Tragic Compensation

Death of a Salesman concludes not with Willy's death, of course, but with its Mass for the Dead, the Requiem, a ritual of final narrative authentication; it is Willy's memorialization. One by one, the four mourners name Willy: first Charley ("Nobody dast blame this man"); then Biff ("the man didn't know who he was"); then Happy ("he had a good dream"); and finally Linda, the remnant of the tragic chorus, who shows us the blindness to which we are all consigned in Willy's end (138–39). Linda is accurate in her elegiac statement that, in her having "made the last payment on the house today ... there'll be nobody home" (139). Just as Willy is buried, as his house is now buried in the great tombstones of apartment buildings surrounding it, down among which no seed will grow, his tragic narrative is formalized and rigid. The family's catharsis is one of narrative ossification. As Krieger points out, "[T]he cathartic principle is ultimately a purely formalistic one, even as tragedy, despite its foreboding rumblings, can retain a force for affirmation through its formal powers alone" (4). Krieger, like Miller, invokes the Nietzschean compensation offered by tragic narrative's response to the tragic vision, which would be unbearable without that compensation. This balance is neither moralistic nor romantic but aesthetic, concerned not so much with the "lesson" of the play as with the aesthetic power of self-ratification.

In response to Willy's blindness, his inability to read his own stories accurately—indeed, his lies about himself and those around him—we must see in Miller's Requiem (as a culmination of the play's tragic vision) a portrayal of the Nietzschean tragic world, one that is "false, cruel, contradictory, destructive, without meaning.... *We have need of lies* in order to conquer this reality, this 'truth,' that is, in order to *live*—That lies are necessary in order to live is itself part of the terrifying and questionable character of existence" (*Will* 853). Willy Loman becomes the fabricator of a tragic truth-narrative out of which he enables those he leaves behind. Willy's stories and the framework Miller provides for them are a Nietzschean compensation for the tragic vision. Miller says that "the very impulse to write springs from an inner chaos crying for order, for meaning, and that meaning must be discovered in the process of writing or the world lies dead" (Introduction 28). In Miller's invocation of the tragic vision, "art is a function of the civilizing act quite as much as the building of the water supply" ("Family" 223). While art, for Nietzsche, is our redemption from negation and nihilism, Miller shows that tragic art is itself redemption from the negation into which tragic insight seems to force us. Willy only glimpses the abjectness of his own illusions: the anagnorisis of *Death of a Salesman* lies in its reader or viewer, for whom tragedy is the tonic and the antidote for anomie and nihilism.

The tragic in *Death of a Salesman* acknowledges the affirmation of life, which is not, finally, Aristotelian catharsis or Hegelian synthesis but what Nietzsche calls "a joyful participation *in tragedy*, as an artistic ritual, which denies and transcends the tragic" (*Birth* 7). In this vision of the tragic, unlike Aristotle's or Hegel's, "understanding" does not occur; Willy sacrifices himself for nothing. This principle is endemic to the contemporary tragic mode, which can be seen, as Krieger says, "using self-destructive crises to force itself to confront the absurdities of earthly reality—those which have always been there lurking beneath for the visionary who would dare give up all to read them." Krieger goes on to say:

[W]e must admit that, at least in our time, driven as it is by crises and 'arrests' and blind as it is to the healing power and saving grace of tragedy, the tragic has come, however unfortunately, to loom as a necessary vision and ... as one that can be neither reduced nor absorbed. (21)

In this way, the unrelenting tragedy of Linda at the end of the play, asking "Why did you do it?" and sobbing as she repeats "We're free" (139), demonstrates the blindness to the healing power of tragedy by which those left behind are driven. In Linda's blindness, a final coda to that of Charley, Biff, and Happy, the intensity of Miller's tragic vision reaches its peak. In the drama, for Miller, lies "the ultimate possibility of raising the truth-consciousness of mankind to a level of such intensity as to transform those who observe it" ("Family" 232). Through Miller's art in *Death of a Salesman* we confront neither the dangers of the success ethic in American business nor the lost self but the critical and tragic notion of the unfindable self in a condition of anomie, struggling through a narrative structure of differentiation and distance. Contrary to Linda's final assertion, Willy—like the rest of us, who feel it less intensely—is not, nor has he ever been, free; he is in a perpetual crisis of authentication predetermined by a rhetorical ground. This ground constitutes itself as the tragic father and the tragic muse he has never known, that chimerical author(ity) figure who is always on the road.

NOTES

1. The Muses, as daughters of Zeus and the Titaness Mnemosyne ("memory"), served a normative cultural role: they were conceived of as a coupling of the heavenly and earthly functions of the fine arts, aspiring to superhuman synthesis and calling on our own human past for their power and effect. The word *muse*, linked to the Latin *mens* (mind, discernment, thought—but also purpose) and our own *mind*, denotes in Greek "memory" or "a reminder," since early poets had no books from which to read and so had to rely on their memories; gradually, the Muses came to be reminders to poets of the rules by which to write properly, of what to write about, and of why those subjects are "worthy." Interestingly and appropriately, in the light of Nietzsche's thought (which I discuss later), while "inspiring" the poet with subjects to be presented in, for example, the Tragic Dionysia, the Muses are associated with Apollo, traditionally their leader.

The so-called Tragic Muse, Melpomene, whose name means "singing," is an appropriate emblematic figure behind *Death of a Salesman*, preoccupied as it is with music and musical form.

2. For Krieger, the tragic vision is nothing less than a view of reality, which inevitably alters with cultural views of reality:

The tragic vision is born *inside* tragedy, as part of it: as a possession of the tragic hero, the vision was a reflection in the realm of thematics of the fully fashioned aesthetic totality which was tragedy. But fearful and even demoniac in its revelations, the vision needed the ultimate soothing power of the aesthetic form which contained it—the tragedy itself—in order to preserve for the world a sanity which the vision itself denied. (3)

The working out of the tragic in a literary form returns a sanity to a maddened world—regulates it (remember Nietzsche's declaration that we have art so that we will not go mad); this passage from Krieger is vital to an understanding of the form of *Salesman*.

3. Anyone irritated by the previous passage on grounds of gender bias should recall that although many of the issues in *Death of a Salesman* are specifically gendered (i.e., pertain to the role of father, mother, son, or a socially conditioned gender-model orientation), many are not; I do not attempt to address the politics here. Note that Miller did not write *Death of a Saleswoman* or *Death of a Salesperson*; concerns specific to men are a central part of the play's thematic weight and of its tragic impetus.

4. *Civilization and Its Discontents* is full of insightful references to this phenomenon, without which the tragic vision is significantly less understandable. Freud's case is that we deny our nature by "naturally" forming ourselves into societies:

> Man's natural aggressive instinct, the hostility of each against all and of all against each, opposes the programme of civilization. This aggressive instinct is the derivative and the main representative of the death instinct which we have found alongside of Eros and which shares world-dominion with it. And now, I think, the meaning of the evolution of civilization is no longer obscure to us. It must present the struggle between Eros and Death, between the instinct of life and the instinct of destruction, as it works itself out in the human species. This struggle is what all life essentially consists of, and the evolution of civilization may therefore be simply described as the struggle for life of the human species. (69)

Each sentence of this passage bears directly on Willy's and Linda's, as well as Biff's, condition, allowing us to achieve a more deeply tragic perspective on it.

5. Some recent studies of social discontent as endemic to Western culture, and particularly as seen in themes of alienation and anomie, bear interestingly on this condition, again as grounds on which the tragic vision is to be built. From Marx to Nietzsche, and then into twentieth-century social and political theory, this issue is central to an understanding of recent social structure. Emile Durkheim, Georg Lukács, and others explore this terrain. A useful source of information on the polar opposition of alienation and anomie, a lack of identity and the lawlessness it breeds, is Gary Thom's *The Human Nature of Discontent: Alienation, Anomie, Ambivalence*, which could serve as the basis of a provocative theoretical investigation of the social structure in *Death of a Salesman* and the condition of all its characters.

6. Willy Loman is Nietzsche's "last man," the low man in an enervated Western culture, the man of little will (willie) whose rhetoric always consists of meaningless dreams of guilt and *ressentiment* and who is unconsciously dominated by a rhetoric of oppression, as opposed to the overman, who, as master of willful rhetoric, does not succumb to the systems of signs he produces but rises above them.

Yet lest we too cleverly try to interpret Willy's name, Miller tells the story, in *Timebends*, of its "discovery": sitting in a showing of Fritz Lang's *Testament of Dr. Mabuse*, Miller was struck by the character of the director of the Sûreté, a "terror-stricken man calling into the void for help that will never come" (178–79). That character's name is Lohmann.

7. Belief in stories is identical to and concealed in belief in "essences." Willy and Hap will not be disillusioned: Brooklyn is rural, Dave Singleman is a god, Biff is a star, Willy is well liked. Indeed, Willy sees himself as déclassé nobility, the essential map, the pioneer, the father, the holder of power, uncorrupted and clean (the language Willy uses to refuse Charley's proffered job shows this self-image clearly (97).

8. See Derrida's discussion of this phenomenon in "Signature Event Context": "a written sign is proffered in the absence of the addressee ..." (315). Further:

> Every sign, linguistic or non-linguistic, spoken or written (in the usual sense of this opposition), as a small or large entity, can be *cited*, put between quotation marks; thereby it can break with every given context, and engender infinitely new contexts in an absolutely nonsaturable fashion. This does not suppose that the mark is valid outside the context, but on the contrary that there are only contexts without any center of absolute anchoring. (320)

9. See Sartre's investigation of the gaze of the other, of the *en-soi* and the *pour-soi* in *Being and Nothingness* (73–84). Willy's desire to be well liked is also a simplified version of Hegel's *schöne Seele*, the "beautiful soul" that is possible only in the synthesis of self and other, the resolution of the conflict of master and slave. In a psychoanalytic context, Anthony Wilden comments on the beautiful soul as being "a consciousness which judges others but which cannot take action on itself in terms of judgement" (289). This is precisely Willy's dilemma: he cannot learn to judge himself or others properly, nor can he take appropriate action in response to self or other.

10. Dave Singleman carries the name of the raw individualist, the singular man who is divorced from society and makes his own way, who is self-reliant, the successful manipulator of the system who can be aloof from life and still be well liked. Singleman is the embodiment of Lukács's view that tragedy is "the full depth of solitude," the struggle between existence and annihilation (56).

APPENDIX I

A measure of the way in which *Death of a Salesman* fits into the Western tragic tradition is the application of Greek terminology to the play. Some of the terms by which, through which, and parallel to which the tragic vision has evolved, and which provide a fruitful context for consideration of writing that claims tragic status, have given me a useful teaching tool to show *Death of a Salesman*'s relation to the tragedy of antiquity. The ways in which the terms apply to *Salesman* are indicated, but by no means exhaustively.

adikia: disruption of the right order (sexual transgression, Willy's lying to Biff about it, general deceit, being poor); see *dike*

arete: virtue (Willy's hypocritical or fictional sense of virtue, adaptable to his
   rhetorical sense of the world)

dike: right order (being well liked, making one's mark, being a success, going
   to Alaska—in particular, taking a risk for big gain; living for one's
   family; knowing the etiquette of the home office, as Howard does)

hamartia: error (Willy's not taking the job offered by Howard, Willy's
   treatment of Charley, not understanding the narrative of the social
   fabric, losing his temper at Biff, suicide)

mimesis: "illusion" or "pretense," as Walter Kaufmann suggests in *Tragedy
   and Philosophy* (33–41), rather than "imitation" or "representation" (the
   style and form of the play)

moira: fate (Willy's misunderstanding of his relationships with Biff and
   himself, Willy's inevitable sinking into self-destruction as a ratifier of
   his already-destroyed self)

Appendix II

A unifying trait in the diverse theories of the tragic since Plato is that they
formulate and portray a cultural crisis that must be resolved, synthesized,
accommodated, eradicated, transcended, acknowledged, suffered—
according to the vicissitudes of the *épistèmé du jour*. The tragic is a dramatic
mechanism for crisis accommodation and authenticity portrayal. Tragedy
affirms some particular view of the issues by which a particular culture sees
and defines itself. Following are sketches of the history of tragic tradition
that I find useful in teaching *Death of a Salesman*.

Plato

Dispersed throughout the *Republic*, Plato's elusive tragic idea relates to the
nature of a proper education. It is a subset of his concerns about poetry and
the state, which must be so tightly controlled in the *paideia*, the body of
knowledge which any properly educated aristocrat must command. The
tragic notion in Plato is to be found in sections 376–403 of the Cornford
translation (see Kaufmann 9–29). Because in Plato all poetry, including the
tragic, must have a didactic and heuristic ground supporting the conservative
and moralistic conception of the *aristos* that Plato is at such pains to support,
it must be "a model of virtuous thoughts" (Plato 75) or must not be tolerated.
Plato would exclude Sophocles's *Antigone* and *Electra*, Euripides's *Medea*,
Hippolytus, *Electra*, and *Trojan Women* from the canon: these works do not
authenticate the vision of humankind that Plato wishes to foster. For the
same reasons, he must have had trouble with Aeschylus's *Oresteia*.

Understanding human beings as rational creatures in danger of irrationality, Plato turned away from the Dionysian origins of the tragic vision, altering it to fit another paradigm or social goal. He would not have known what to make of Willy Loman and his chimerical *paideia*.

Aristotle

Asking students to reread parts of the *Poetics* (particularly 1449a.7–1455a.19) in the context of tragic authentication leads to the interesting realization that Aristotle's project is much more like Plato's than one might have thought. It is also important to remember that Aristotle is almost incomprehensibly vague in his definition of the tragic: he does not explain any of the key terms on which he models that theory; of course, this is a reason for his lasting influence on changing ideas of tragedy.

For Aristotle the tragic is a catharsis of fear and pity that the audience of tragedy feels in the presence of a good person's sufferings; through the character's anagnorisis we see our own shortcomings and their possible transcendence. We identify with such characters as they cross the threshold of realizing that they are indeed human. For Aristotle this threshold of recognition and discovery requires unity in and concentration by the audience of tragedic drama. Catharsis is a quieting, a distancing of personal and cosmic discomfort at the level of the viewer. In Aristotle's stress on "action" (which we might now call theme) and plot over character (e.g., Miller's references to the Salesman rather than to Willy by name), he counters Plato's view of tragic poetry—as depicting the good person doing good—by introducing the central concept of hamartia, the tragic error or misjudgment by which the heroic individual must be made to gain insight into the nature of the Logos. It is ironic that Aristotle, rather than Plato, is held to initiate the concentration on the tragic hero in Western literature and drama; he would have been displeased at this perception. Aristotle was concerned with the integration of the whole, with the organic unity of humankind with all other things in a condition of ordered, analytical structure.

To Aristotle tragedy concerns itself with *eleos* (pity or mercy) and *phobos* (fear), but we may only speculate on how he intended them to interrelate, if indeed he did, and how they fit into a cathartic context. The *Poetics* is simply too allusive and unclear. What is clear in Aristotle's thought is that the point of tragedy, toward which all the formal elements of the drama work, is to arouse and purge certain emotions. According to Aristotle, Sophocles's *Oedipus Tyrannus* represents the highest instance of this function, since it shows the purest and most powerful form of this cultural normalization and the assertive emplacement of the order of the Logos (Aristotle does not mention that *Oedipus Tyrannus* won only second prize in the Summer Dionysia; apparently the audience was not behaving in proper Aristotelian fashion).

Both Plato's and Aristotle's notions of the tragic, severely limiting in terms of what can properly be called tragedy, are moralistic and didactic. They see the role of tragedy as offering a lesson to society in general on what constitutes its best interests. That is, both Plato and Aristotle take a generalist view of the cultural authentication that tragedy as a public spectacle offers.

Medieval and Renaissance Tragedy

The idea of tragedy becomes even more programmatic in its medieval (Catholic-Christian) form—as demonstrated, for example, in Boccaccio and Chaucer, who deal with the inevitable fall of illustrious men. In medieval tragedy, the trappings of the world are undermined and the lesson of humility and obedience taught. Tragedy becomes an authentication of the Christian cosmos and of humankind's place in it.

When we teach Renaissance tragedy, we tend to make the most of its developments over medieval models, with its creation of the exuberant "modern" notion of *humanitas*, the power and energy of individual man, but Renaissance tragedies from Thomas Kyd through William Shakespeare and Ben Jonson also work as moral exempla, urging attendance to the lessons of the consequences of evil (with two great exceptions: Christopher Marlowe's *Dr. Faustus* and Shakespeare's *King Lear*). This complex and familiar tragic drama is an exuberant exercise in the authentication of a new sense of the self as confined by Providence but holding immense powers of observation and action, uneasy in its role as subservient to externals but still obeying (as in *Hamlet*).

Hegel

With Hegel's idea of the tragic, explored in *The Philosophy of Fine Art* (particularly 1: 272–313; 2: 213–15; 4: 295–303, 308–26, 330–42) though never developed into a concerted theory, several new elements of tragedy as cultural authentication appear. Hegel's view of tragedy entails a new urgency concerning the human condition: the sundering of the social from the particular in human experience, inherent in Renaissance *humanitas*, reaches critical proportions in Hegel's dialectical philosophy. A person cannot act on one plane at a time, cannot be an individual and a collective being simultaneously, and so is tragic. Tragedy in Hegel destroys the individual but reconciles the dialectical position from which that destruction takes place. Individuals destroy themselves though the rigid one-sidedness of their characters, or they must identify themselves with a course of action to which they are fundamentally opposed. For Hegel tragedy, then, is the collision of opposing positions that are reconciled by the tragedy itself, by the portrayal of that collision and reconciliation. The most significant action in the tragic mode is the presentation of the tragic reconciliation itself. Ancient tragedies—the best of which is, for Hegel, not *Oedipus* but *Antigone*—portray the collision of ethical positions; modern tragedies should portray humanity as inwardly torn, self-centered, ripped apart by the forces driving the tragic vision (one can readily see the seeds of Miller's notion of Willy's self-sundering in the Hegelian tragic view). Tragedy now is a reconciliation into unity of the moral and ethical substance of Aristotle's hamartia in the hero. Hegel calls this principle the "too-assertive particularity" of the tragic figure, who is made heroic by this particularity. It is ironic that Hegel's view is the basis of modern existential tragedy, in which the particular has become the alienated and disenfranchised, for to Hegel the aim of tragedy, like all art, is the revelation of the eternal and divine in sensible form. Tragedy again teaches its lesson of order and structure and of the need for self-authentication in terms of this order. The Hegelian universe remains serenely and implacably calm in the face of human tragic furor.

Nietzsche

Nietzsche develops a radically different sense of the tragic, starting in *The Birth of Tragedy* and continuing through his later works, out of Hegel's dialectical sense and Schopenhauer's response to it. Schopenhauer's development of the tragic vision undermines and destroys Hegel's. For Schopenhauer, humanity is tragic because it is born human: our condition itself is tragic. The tragic is the acknowledgment of the "unspeakable pain, the wretchedness and misery of mankind, the triumph of wickedness, the scornful mastery of chance, and the irretrievable fall of the just and the innocent" (1: 253). Since to Schopenhauer the world, and the human life that is its measure, can never give satisfaction and therefore is not worthy of our affection, the tragic anagnorisis leads to resignation in the face of futility.

Nietzsche categorically rejects this idea, reversing Schopenhauerian resignation and stasis. For Nietzsche the tragic vision is one in which we experience tragedy in the living of life; by affirming the dichotomy of joy and suffering that defines life, we achieve tragic insight. In section 7 of *The Birth of Tragedy*, Nietzsche declares that we must look boldly right into the "terrible destructiveness" of nature, where we will see neither Hegelian synthesis nor Schopenhauerian stasis but a dramatic glimpse of the gulf between "the real truth of nature and the lie of culture that poses as if it were the only reality" (*Birth* 8).

Nietzsche reverses not only Hegel and Schopenhauer but all of tragic tradition back to Plato, as indeed is his goal. By exposing the "lie of culture" on which tragic visions have been posited, Nietzsche declares a new sense of life itself. As he develops it throughout his writing, Nietzsche shows us a tragic world with no orderly structure but opposing forces, a world of chaos, without laws, reason, or purpose. These forces are superadded by humankind, that "clever beast who invented knowing" ("On Truth" 79). To be tragic is to glimpse the truth of human nature, which is the chaos of its joy and suffering. The world of laws and systems, of love or success or business acumen or religion, that orderly and purposeful world we posit around us, is an illusion (a mimesis) that we have erected to keep the "real world" out; that real world goes on in its chaos without us, without acknowledgment of our "views, values, and our desires" (Nehamas 43). While we see the world revealed in its fearfulness, however, we see nature itself; this shock of recognition, which the tragic shows us, has nothing to do with nobility or transgression, with sin or hamartia or hubris, but reveals the universal joy and suffering in the interplay of forces defining life. Our culture rejects the real world in favor of a predictable one over which we pretend to have some control.

Nietzsche declares that Aristotle's notion of *katharsis* is simply not borne out by human experience: in the presence of fear-inducing action, we are not relieved of our fears but maintain and deepen them. "Aristotle's great misunderstanding," Nietzsche says, "is believing the tragic affects to be two *depressive* effects, terror and pity. If he were right, tragedy would be an art dangerous to life: one would have to warn against it as notorious and a public danger" (*Will* 851). For Nietzsche tragedy is a tonic, reminding us of our chaotic existence. It is, in other words, a cultural (individual and collective) self-authentication frightfully complicated by our lack of a self, as we generally define it, to authenticate. Nietzsche's affirmation of the tragic in the new context he creates for it is the tragic watershed for my interpretation of *Death of a Salesman*.

CHRISTOPHER BIGSBY

Arthur Miller: Poet

In the Church of the Holy Trinity in Stratford Upon Avon, in England, there is an inscription that I especially like. On the tombstone marking the burial place of William Shakespeare are the words "William Shakespeare Poet." This is not because he was the author of poetry, which he was, or because he wrote in that most basic rhythm of the English language, iambics, but because his was an art whose language, whose characters, whose metaphoric allusiveness lifted present fact into universal significance. I also take that inscription to be a reminder of the origins of drama, born out of the rib of poetry, to be an indication of the metaphoric force of the theater. I also warm to the implication that in Shakespeare's age the title "poet" was not only a badge of honor but the mark of a man seen as a chronicler of the age and a force in the land.

An odd way to start a lecture on Arthur Miller, you might think, a man who, especially in this country, is so often praised, and occasionally decried, for what is taken to be his realism, a realism expressed through the authentic prose of a salesman, a longshoreman, a businessman. This, after all, is the Arthur Miller who observed that in America a poet is seen as being "like a barber trying to erect a skyscraper." He is, in other words, regarded as being "of no consequence." Yet I want to suggest not merely that Arthur Miller is no simple realist and hasn't been for fifty years but that he is incontestably a

From *Michigan Quarterly Review* 37, no. 4 (Fall 1998). © 1998 by the University of Michigan.

poet, one who sees the private and public worlds as one, who is a chronicler of the age and a creator of metaphors.

In an essay on realism, written in 1997, Miller made a remark that I find compellingly interesting. "Willy Loman," he said, "is not a real person. He is if I may say so a figure in a poem." That poem is not simply the language he or the other characters speak, though this is shaped, charged with a muted eloquence of a kind which he has said was not uncommon in their class half a century or more ago. Nor is it purely a product of the stage metaphors which, like Tennessee Williams, he presents as correlatives of the actions he elaborates. The poem is the play itself and *hence* the language, the mise en scène, the characters who glimpse the lyricism of a life too easily ensnared in the prosaic, a life which aspires to metaphoric force.

Willy Loman a figure in a poem? What kind of a figure? A metaphor. A metaphor is the meeting point of disparate elements brought together to create meaning. Willy Loman's life is just such a meeting point, containing, as it does, the contradictions of a culture whose dream of possibility has foundered on the banality of its actualization, a culture that has lost its vision of transcendence, earthing its aspirations so severely in the material world. As Miller has said of Willy's speech when he confronts his employer, Howard, a speech which he rightly calls an "aria," "what we have is the story of a vanished era, part real, part imaginary, the disappearing American dream of mutuality and in its place the terrible industrial process that discards people like used up objects. And to me this is poetic and it is realism both." So it is, and much the same could be said of the rest of his work. It grows out of an awareness of the actual but that actuality is reshaped, charged with a significance that lifts it into a different sphere.

But let's, very briefly, look at some of the component elements that shape Arthur Miller's poetry in *Death of a Salesman*. In a notebook he once remarked that "there is a warehouse of scenery in a telling descriptive line." So there is. Consider the opening stage direction to Act 1, an act, incidentally, that has a bracketed subtitle, "An Overture," and which begins with music. The description, the first words of the text, is at once descriptive and metaphoric. "A melody," we are told, "is heard, playing upon a flute. It is small and fine, telling of grass and trees and the horizon." This is something of a challenge to a composer but what follows is equally a challenge to a designer as he describes a house that is simultaneously real and imagined, a blend of fact and memory which precisely mirrors the frame of mind of its protagonist and the nature of the dreams that he seeks, Gatsby-like, to embrace.

In other words, both in terms of music and stage set we are dealing immediately with the real and with a poetic image, with a poet's gesture, and that is how it was seen by a young Lanford Wilson who, in 1955, saw a student production. It was, he has said, "the most magical thing I'd ever seen in my life ... the clothesline from the old building all around the house gradually faded into big, huge beech trees. I nearly collapsed. It was the most extraordinary scenic effect and, of course, I was hooked on theater from that moment ... that magic was what I was always drawn to." And as yet, of course, not a word of the text has been spoken, though a great deal has been communicated as the real has been transmuted into symbol. And, incidentally, an astonishing number of playwrights have acknowledged this play as being central to them. Tony Kushner was drawn to the theater by watching his mother perform in it. David Rabe virtually borrows lines from it in *Sticks and Bones*, Lorraine Hansberry acknowledged its influence on *A Raisin in the Sun* while Adrienne Kennedy has confessed to constantly rereading it and keeping a notebook of Miller's remarks about theater. David Margulies first read it at the age of eleven and later, somewhat controversially, wrote a play called *The Loman Family Picnic*. Tom Stoppard saw *Salesman* as a major influence on his first play while Vaclav Havel has likewise acknowledged its inspirational power. But for the moment let's stay with the set.

As Miller said in the notebook he kept while writing *Salesman*, "Modern life has broken out of the living room. Just as it was impossible for Shakespeare to say his piece in the confines of a church, so today Shaw's living room is an anachronism. The object of scene design," he continued, "ought not to reference a locale but to raise it into a significant statement."

The original stage direction indicated of the Loman house that "it had once been surrounded by open country, but it was now hemmed in with apartment houses. Trees that used to shade the house against the open sky and hot summer sun were for the most part dead or dying." Jo Mielziner's job, as designer and lighting engineer, was to realize this in practical terms, but it is already clear from Miller's description that the set is offered as a metaphor, a visual marker of social and psychological change. It is not only the house that has lost its protection, witnessed the closing down of space, not only the trees that are withering away and dying with the passage of time. It is a version of America. It is human possibility. It is Willy Loman.

Other designers have come up with other solutions to the play's challenges, as they have to Mielziner's use of back-lit unbleached muslin, on which the surrounding tenement buildings were painted and which could therefore be made to appear and disappear at will. Other designers have found equivalents to his use of projection units which could surround the Loman house with trees whose spring leaves would stand as a reminder of the springtime of Willy's life, at least as recalled by a man determined to romanticize a past when, he likes to believe, all was well with his life.

Fran Thompson, designer of London's National Theatre production in 1996, chose to create an open space with a tree at center stage, but a tree whose trunk had been sawn through leaving a section missing, the tree being no more literal and no less substantial than Willy's memories.

And, indeed, it is the fact that for the most part this is a play which takes place in the mind and memory of its central character which determines its form as past and present interact in his mind, linked together by visual, verbal or aural rhymes. In the National Theatre production, all characters remained on stage throughout, being animated when they moved into the forefront of Willy's troubled mind, or swung into view on a revolve. The space, in other words, while literal was simultaneously an image of a mind haunted by memories, seeking connections.

Meanwhile, despite his emphasis on "the actual" and "the real," the language of *Death of a Salesman* is not simply the transcribed speech of 1930s Brooklyn, though its author is aware that all speech has its particular rhythms, aware, too, that, as he has said, "the Lomans have gotten accustomed to elevating their way of speaking." "Attention, attention must be finally paid to such a person," was not, as Mary McCarthy and others thought, an inadvertent revelation of a concealed Jewish identity but Miller's deliberate attempt to underscore the exemplary significance of Willy Loman, for, as he said, "prose is the language of family relations; it is the inclusion of the larger world beyond that naturally opens a play to the poetic." And, indeed, Linda's despairing cry is that of a wife claiming significance for a desperate husband abandoned by those whose opinions he values, as it is also that of a woman acknowledging that that husband is the embodiment of other suffering human beings.

And if Miller was right in saying that "in the theater the poetic does not depend, at least not wholly, on poetic language," there is no doubt that the poetic charge to his language is carefully worked for. And which playwright, American or European, has offered such a range of different varieties of speech: a Brooklyn longshoreman, a 17th century farmer, a Yankee carpenter, each authentic but each shaped so that there are moments when it sings. Turn to the notebooks which he kept while writing *The Crucible* and you will find a number of speeches tried out first in verse. Here is one of them.

We have exalted charity over malice
Suspicion above trust
We have hung husbands for loyalty
To wives, and honored traitors to their families
And now even the fields complain.
There will be hunger in Massachusetts

This winter the plowman is busy
Spying on his brother, and the earth
Gone to seed. A wilderness of weeds
Is claiming the pastures of our world
We starve for a little charity.
... nothing will grow but dead things.

Even in *Death of a Salesman* Charley's final speech was first tried out in a loose free verse.

A man who doesn't build anything must be liked
He must be cheerful on bad days
Even calamities mustn't break through
Cause one thing, he has got to be liked.
He doesn't tell the law, or give you medicines
So there's no rock bottom to your life.
All you know [is] that on good days or bad,
You gotta come in cheerful.
No calamity must be permitted to break through
Cause one thing, always you're a man who's gotta be liked.
You're way out there riding on a smile and a shoeshine
And when they start not smilin' back,
It's the big catastrophe. And then you get
A couple of spots on your hat, and you're finished
Cause there's no rock bottom to your life.

In the final version it loses its free verse form and its redundancies but retains its lyrical charge. The tension in the prose, the rhythms, the images, meanwhile, were born out of a poetic imagination. It is spoken in prose but a prose charged with the poetic.

If Willy Loman was a figure in a poem, that is even more true of the pseudonymous character in Miller's new play, *Mr. Peters' Connections*, set in what the opening stage direction calls "a broken structure indicating an old abandoned night club in New York City." But that stage direction is itself metaphoric for it is not the setting alone that is a "broken structure." It is, potentially, a life. And if this play is a poem it is, in part, an elegy, an elegy for an individual but also, in some senses, for a culture, for a century, indeed for human existence itself.

For as he said the questions theater tries to address are "death and betrayal and injustice and how we are to account for this little life of ours."

In a sense these are the subjects of *Mr. Peters' Connections*, though it is not a play that ends in despair.

It is a play which laments the loss of youth, the stilling of urgencies, the dulling of intensity, as love, ambition, utopian dreams devolve into little more than habit and routine. It is a play about loss, the loss of those connections that once seemed so self-evident as moment led to moment, as relationships gave birth to their own meaning, as the contingent event shaped itself into coherent plot, as the fact of the journey implied a purposeful direction and a desirable destination. It is about a deracinated man, literally a man who has lost his sense of roots, his connections. In another sense it is a contemplation of life itself whose intensity and coherence slowly fades, whose paradox can never finally be resolved, as it is also a confrontation with death.

Mr. Peters' Connections is about a man at the end of his life who feels things slipping away from him. The conversations which constitute the play are the visions of a man in that half world between wakefulness and sleep for whom life drifts away, becomes a jumble of half-forgotten people, incomplete stories. One by one he summons those with whom he has shared his life, but he encounters them at first as strangers, as if they had already passed beyond the sphere in which he exists. A one-time lover, a brother, a daughter, they appear and disappear but he can never quite recall what they were to him or he to them. In some senses their identity doesn't matter. Yet he knows they must hold a clue to the meaning of his existence. The question is, what did he derive from them? What was important? What was the subject?

Chekhov sub-titled *The Cherry Orchard* a "comedy," and there is something of Chekhov here, something of his ironies. That play ends with a man on his own in a room, the meaning of his life on the verge of dissolving. Mr. Peters' connections are similarly disappearing, his connections to others, to himself, to a structure of meaning.

For Willy Loman, meaning always lay in the future. His life was "kind of temporary" as he awaited the return of his father, Godot-like, to flood his life with meaning or as he projected a dream of tomorrow that would redeem his empty and troubling present. In *Mr. Peters' Connections* meaning lies not in the future but the past, in memories that even now are dulling like the embers of a once-bright fire, in the lives of those others who, in dying, take with them pieces of the jigsaw, fragments of the world whose clarity of outline has been a product of shared assumptions, mutual apprehensions. What happens, he implicitly asks himself, to our sense of ourselves and the world when one by one our fellow witnesses withdraw their corroboration, when there is nobody left to say, "yes, that's the way it was, that's who you once were." As they die and withdraw from the stage they take incremental elements of meaning with them, gradually thin his sense of the real to transparency.

In a sense *Mr. Peters' Connections* is not set anywhere. The night club had once been a cafeteria, a library, a bank, its function shifting as the supposed solidities of the past dissolve. In a way, compacted into this place is the history of New York, the history of a culture and of a man. It exists in the emotional memory of its protagonist.

The word "connections" refers not only to his links with other people, particularly those closest to him, but also to his desire to discover the relationship between the past and the present, between simple event and the meaning of that event. In other words he is in search of a coherence that will justify life to itself. In facing the fact of death he is forced to ask himself what life has meant, what has been its subject. In that context the following is a key speech and one in which I find a justification for Miller's own approach to drama as well as to the process of living which that drama both explores and celebrates: "I do enjoy the movies, but every so often I wonder, 'what was the *subject* of the picture?' I think that's what I'm trying to ... to ... find my connection with is ... what's the word ... *continuity* ... yes with the past, perhaps ... in the hope of finding a ... yes, a subject. That's the idea I think." In other words, the simplest of questions remains the most necessary of questions "what is it all for?"

Fifty years ago, in the notebook he kept while writing *Death of a Salesman*, he wrote the following: "Life is formless ... its interconnections are concealed by lapses of time, by events occurring in separated places, by the hiatus of memory.... Art suggests or makes these interconnections palpable. Form is the tension of these interconnections, man with man, man with the past and present environment. The drama at its best is the mass experience of this tension." *Death of a Salesman* was concerned with that and generated a form commensurate with its subject. Much the same could be said of *Mr. Peters' Connections*.

It is tempting to see a relationship between the protagonist and his creator. Mr. Peters recalls a time of mutuality and trust, a time when the war against fascism gave people a sense of shared endeavor. Once, he recalls, his generation believed in "saving the world." "What's begun to haunt me," he explained, "is that next to nothing I have believed has turned out to be true. Russia, China, and very often America...." In a conversation, three years ago, with Vaclav Havel, Miller himself remarked, "I am a deeply political person; I became that way because of the time I grew up in, which was the Fascist period.... I thought ... that Hitler ... might well dominate Europe, and maybe even have a tremendous effect on America, and I couldn't imagine having an audience in the theater for two hours and not trying to enlist them in some spiritual resistance to this awful thing." Later, when China went communist, he set himself to oppose McCarthyism. He once confessed that he had thought that theater could "change the world." Today, like Mr. Peters, he is, perhaps, less sure of such an easy redemption.

If in some senses Mr. Peters is contemplating death, there is more than one form of dying. The loss of vision, of a sense of transcendent values, of purpose, what he calls a subject, is another form of death, operative equally on the metaphysical, social and personal level. As Peters remarks, "most of the founding fathers were all Deists ... they believed that God had wound up the world like a clock and then disappeared. We are unwinding now, the ticks further and further apart. So instead of tick-tick-tick-tick we've got tick (pause) tick (pause) tick. And we get bored between ticks, and boredom is a form of dying...." The answer, perhaps, lies in a realization that there is no hierarchy of meaning. As another character tells him, "everything is relevant! You are trying to pick and choose what is important ... like a batter waiting for a ball he can hit. But what if you have to happily swing at everything they thrust at you?" In other words, perhaps one can do no more than live with intensity, acknowledge the simultaneous necessity for and vulnerability of those connections without which there is neither private meaning nor public morality.

Willy Loman believed that the meaning of his life was external to himself, blind to the fact that he already contained that meaning, blind to the love of his wife and son. Mr. Peters comes to understand that his life, too, *is* its meaning, his connections *are* what justifies that life. This play, then, is not about a man ready to run down the curtain, to succumb to the attraction of oblivion. He may not rage against the dying of the light but he does still find a reason to resist the blandishments of the night. So it is that Mr. Peters, former airline pilot, remarks that "when you've flown into hundreds of gorgeous sunsets, you want them to go on forever and hold off the darkness."

What is the poem? It is Mr. Peters' life, as it is the play itself which mimics, symbolizes, offers a metaphor for that search for coherence and meaning that is equally the purpose of art and the essence of life.

Last year Don DeLillo published *Underworld*. It was, in part, an account of America in the era of the Cold War. It was 827 pages long. Norman Mailer explored the psyche of Lee Harvey Oswald and the culture which formed him in 791 pages. Thomas Pynchon took us back into America's past, its divisions and coherences, in *Mason and Dixon*, a book which ran to 773 pages. Willem de Kooning has spoken of the burden that Americanness places on the American artist. That burden seems to be, at least in part, a desire to capture the culture whole, to find an image commensurate with the size and nature of its ambitions, its dreams, its flawed utopianism, whether it be Melville trying to harpoon a society in search of its own meaning, Dreiser convinced that the accumulation of detail will edge him closer to truth, or John Dos Passos offering to throw light on the USA by means of the multiple viewpoints of modernism. A big country demands big books. James Michener tried to tackle it state by state, with a preference for the larger ones. Gore Vidal worked his way diachronically, president by president, in books which if strung together would run into thousands of pages and in which he hoped to tell the unauthorized biography of a society. Henry James called the novel a great baggy monster and that is what it has proved to be in the hands of American novelists. Even America's poets, from Whitman through to Ashbery, have shown a fondness for the epic.

The dramatist inhabits an altogether different world, unless your name is Eugene O'Neill, whose *Strange Interlude* ran for six hours, including a dinner break. He or she is limited, particularly in the modern theater, to no more than a couple of hours. Increasingly, indeed, he is limited as to the number of actors he can deploy and the number of sets he can call for. The theater, of course, is quite capable of turning the few into many and a single location into multiple settings but the pressure is toward concision. The 800 page book becomes a 100 page play text. The pressure, in other words, is toward a kind of poetry, not the poetry of Christopher Fry or T. S. Eliot, but a poetry generated out of metaphor, a language without excess, a language to be transmuted into physical form, the word made flesh. Miller collapses the history of his society into the lives of his characters and in doing so exemplifies a truth adumbrated by Ralph Waldo Emerson a century and a half ago when he said that, "We are always coming up with the emphatic facts of history in our private experience and verifying them here ... in other words there is properly no history, only biography." Miller does not need 800 pages. He captures the history of a culture, indeed human existence itself, in the life of an individual, indeed in a single stage direction.

At the beginning of *Death of a Salesman* Willy Loman enters carrying two suitcases. It takes the whole play and him a lifetime to realize that they are not just the marks of his calling. They are the burden of his life, a life that he will lay down not just for his sons but for a faith as powerful and all-consuming as any that has ever generated misguided martyrs. Staring into the future, in his present, he carries the burden of the past. He is, for a moment, the compacted history of a people, the embodiment of a myth, a figure in a poem, the poem of America, with its thousand points of light, its New Eden, its city on a hill, its manifest destiny. Here, distilled in a single stage image, is the essence of a whole culture still clinging to a faith that movement equals progress, selling itself a dream that accepts that personal and national identity are a deferred project and that tomorrow will bring epiphany, revelation.

Willy Loman had all the wrong dreams but they were a country's dreams instilled into him out there in the heartland where his father, also a salesman, set out on that endless American journey into possibility, unmindful of those he abandoned, his eyes on the prize, a moment never forgotten by his son who constantly hears the sound of the flutes his father made and sold. For those who watch his dilemma, that sound, like the shrinking space around the Loman home, as a subtle light change takes us from past to present, recalls hope and betrayal in the same instant, in a compacted metaphor, the hope and betrayal seen by America's writers from Cooper and Twain to Fitzgerald and beyond.

The subtitle of *Death of a Salesman* is *Certain Private Conversations in Two Acts and a Requiem*. Those private conversations are conducted in Willy Loman's mind but they are also America's conversation with itself. Fifty years later, in *Mr. Peters' Connections*, comes another such series of conversations as a man looks back over his life and wonders what it may have amounted to, what connections there are between people, between event and consequence, between the present and the past which it contains. He, too, is a figure in a poem. The poem is his life and he its author, but not he alone, for, as virtually all of Miller's plays suggest, meaning is not something that will one day cohere. It is not an ultimate revelation. It is not contained within the sensibility of an isolated self. It lies in the connections between people, between actions and their effects, between then and now. The true poetry is that which springs into being as each individual acknowledges responsibility not for themselves alone but for the world they conspire in creating and for those with whom they share past and present. The poetry which Arthur Miller writes and the poetry which he celebrates is the miracle of human life, in all its bewilderments, its betrayals, its denials, but, finally, and most significantly, its transcendent worth.

Arthur Miller is almost eighty-three. You could be forgiven for not believing that, since his new play is the fourth he has written in the present decade, more than he has written in any other since the 1930s when he was creating his first works as a student back in Michigan. He will probably live for ever but if he doesn't I would, finally, here like to claim the presumption of suggesting the words that should one day be carved on any memorial. There should be just three of them. They should read, Arthur Miller Poet.

COLBY H. KULLMAN

Death of a Salesman *at Fifty:*
An Interview with Arthur Miller

*D*eath *of a Salesman* had its first public performance at the Locust Street Theater in Philadelphia. In his autobiography, *Timebends*, Arthur Miller recalls that directly across the street the Philadelphia Orchestra was performing Beethoven's Seventh Symphony that afternoon, and the play's director, Elia Kazan, thought it might be a good idea to expose Lee J. Cobb, who played Willy Loman, to the majesty and exuberance of the music to inspire him for the ordeal to come:

> We were now aware that Willy's part was among the longest in dramatic literature, and Lee was showing signs of wearying. We sat on either side of him in a box, inviting him, as it were, to drink of the heroism of that music, to fling himself into his role tonight without holding back. We thought of ourselves, still, as a kind of continuation of a long and undying past.

Whatever stirred the spirit in Cobb, he did perform mightily, along with the rest of the cast, and from that night forward audiences and critics have praised the play as precisely that "continuation of a long and undying past" stretching from the Greek theater to the present day.

From *Michigan Quarterly Review* 37, no. 4 (Fall 1998): 624-634. © Colby H. Kullman.

It is hoped that the aura of *Salesman* in its 50th year enhances and does not erase the accomplishments of Arthur Miller during the last decade, when new plays and revivals have kept his words before audiences around the world. One thinks of the Roundabout Theater's 1992 revival of *The Price*, the National Actors Theater's production of *The Crucible*, the 1994 Olivier Best Play Award for the London production of *Broken Glass*, and the successful 1996 Nicholas Hytner film version of *The Crucible*. During the summer of 1997, the Williamstown Theater Festival staged *All My Sons* (directed by Barry Edelstein) and *The Ride Down Mount Morgan* (directed by Scott Elliott); shortly thereafter these productions moved to New York City. In October of 1997, the Signature Theatre Company in New York opened its season with *The American Clock* (directed by James Houghton) and concluded a year of Miller plays with a new work, *Mr. Peters' Connections* (directed by Garry Hynes). Meanwhile a revival of *A View from the Bridge* at the Roundabout Theater Company, directed by Michael Mayer, introduced this play to a new generation of viewers. The enthusiasm of these young directors, all in their thirties, contributed, in part, to the success of these productions.

This is only the tip of the iceberg, however. In high schools and colleges, in small towns and large cities all over the world, people are discovering daily the power of Arthur Miller's plays. If *Salesman* remains the flagship of his great career, a score of other dramatic pieces continue to link "a long and undying past" to the present moment of the contemporary stage.

On September 17, 1997, I interviewed Arthur Miller in his East Side, New York City apartment. The occasion provided the playwright with the opportunity to talk about *Death of a Salesman* fifty years after its successful Broadway premiere on 10 February 1949. Although the interview focused on *Salesman*, Miller was free to take the conversation in any direction he felt suitable.

KULLMAN: *Death of a Salesman* will soon be fifty years old. What are your thoughts at this time about your masterpiece?

MILLER: One thing that strikes me now has occurred to me from time to time. I directed *Death of a Salesman* in China and I also directed it in Stockholm in Swedish. The reactions of casts and audiences, with a few very small differences, are the same as with other productions around the world. Since *Salesman* is involved so intimately with American civilization (it seems like the completely American play), how true is it that these cultures are all that different? Some of the etiquette is different. People don't address parents quite the way Americans do, and there is also a question of intimacy. Americans make a play at being very intimate very quickly, which seems disrespectful sometimes to people who aren't used to instant emotional closeness. For example, in China, in the scene where one of the brothers (they're both seemingly asleep), asks the other whether he's sleeping, the Chinese find that very strange. I said, "Why is that strange?" They replied, "It would be impolite to awaken him." Every play shows cultural idiosyncrasies in a foreign production, but I was pleased at how the main thrust of the play becomes very Swedish or very Chinese.

KULLMAN: You describe in *Timebends* a Chinese man coming up to you and saying, "It's what we all want, the dream, to have it all." Coming from a communist country, doesn't such a comment seem strange?

MILLER: It makes me wonder every time it opens in another country. How will the play be understood or misunderstood?

KULLMAN: Madrid, not known for its liberal politics, had a very famous production of *Salesman*, too, didn't it?

MILLER: They've had several over the years. Whole generations of actors have come and gone, riding on that shoeshine. One question that keeps rising in my mind is what really are the cultural differences among people.

KULLMAN: There's just been an African-American cast of *Salesman* which performed at New Stage Theater in Jackson, Mississippi. And I know that *After the Fall* was done with a black actress some time ago in London. Recently, August Wilson and Robert Brustein debated interracial cross-casting of plays. Brustein was in favor and Wilson was very much against having white people play black parts in his plays. How do you feel about all-black productions of *Salesman*?

MILLER: The first of those was at least twenty-five years ago in Baltimore.

KULLMAN: Did it work?

MILLER: Well, it didn't, I didn't think. I went down to see it, but the actors weren't that good. It had nothing to do with race. When the acting is terrific, the whole thing works. But that's true whether they're white or black or Chinese. If you put on a lousy production with white actors, it's lousy. There is a problem, or can be, at this stage of our social evolution, with mixing the casts. It may not be a question of race so much as class. You would rarely find a black man in a high executive position where he was swinging his weight around. There would always be the lingering question of how could this possibly happen? Or, reversing the field, let's suppose you were going to do O'Neill's *The Emperor Jones*, and you decided you were going to use a white actor in the central role and black actors in other roles, what happens to the play? Wilson has a point. I think he's got an agenda that's political and immoral. But there is a real question about cross-casting. I don't think you can give a blanket answer. I can see where you can play a black Hamlet if he were an original enough actor. James Earl Jones could have done it. I would believe him because his emotional range is so profound. It's hard enough on a white actor. When he's got to overcome the social barriers of color, at the same time, he's got to be almost twice as good doing the role.

KULLMAN: And it seems in August Wilson's plays a lot is directed toward the situation of the African American family in America, so racial appearance and identity become much more important.

MILLER: It's very tangled. There's no single answer.... I guess *Salesman's* ability to somehow transcend the moment that it was written in has contributed to its long-lasting success, but that's really an enigma to start with. You see, that play was written in 1948, when we were starting the biggest boom in the history of the United States. However, a good part of the population, including me and President Truman, were prepared for another depression. We had only escaped the first depression by the advent of war. It was, I think, a year and a half into the war before we absorbed all the unemployed; therefore, what were all these young guys going to do when they came home? There had to be another crisis. We turned out to be completely cockeyed. The fact of the matter is that the Marshall Plan supplied the cash to Europe to consume everything we could manufacture. The boom began that way. We were the only real money in the world. Every other European currency was weak, worthless in some cases. We were the sole Empire. I don't think any of us had foreseen that. Probably a lot of people had, but I didn't know about it.

Salesman appeared in '49 in a country already starting to prosper, and to take a completely unforeseen path. The psychology of the audience was still that of depression people. The depression had only ended maybe ten years earlier, and people were on very shaky ground for the following ten years because of the war and the uncertainty as to how the country and the economy were going to go. I won't even mention our situation with Russia. The atmosphere was filled with uncertainty at the moment, but a growing prosperity. When considering the income of Willy Loman, we're talking about a world that already was disappearing. Indeed, I can tell you that I myself had difficulty at one point placing this play in its proper time. I kept being surprised by Biff's reference to being at war because it seemed to me later that this play had taken place before the war.

KULLMAN: It is 1942 and then 1928. There is very little about the war in the play; and at this time the war must have been a major force in the lives of everyone.

MILLER: So it's already suspended in time, a little bit off the earth. It's not a documentary of a period and never tried to be. Consequently, it escaped a period feeling, I suppose, because I keep getting the same astonished report from people that it seems to have been written yesterday.

KULLMAN: This past Sunday [15 September 1997], the *New York Times* ran an article about four young directors, all in their thirties, who are working with various Arthur Miller plays produced in New York during 1997; and they all explain why your plays work for them, but the article doesn't ask you.

MILLER: A mystery involved here. As a writer, I've always believed that while my work and I myself are embedded in whatever period I am writing about, clearly I am sensitive to the winds that are blowing in the culture. At the same time, I have always felt that the issue was not to deal with the problem in the abstract, but to deal with the people who are *in* that problem. The emphasis is on the people. The general problem begins to resolve itself even before the play is finished.

KULLMAN: Many viewers feel that they see something of their fathers as well as some of themselves in the character of Willy Loman. Willy seems to be a universal type, and his fate continues to fascinate us.

MILLER: Of course, I couldn't be more pleased that the play has endured. I think that if it is easy to understand why a play has endured, it won't endure. If you can explain it in two sentences, then it has the appearance of a rigid formula and falls apart. I think from the outset, from the day I wrote it, certainly from the day it was first performed, its temporal situation was already quite uncertain. It was to me anyway, and I think it was very quickly to a lot of people. The play ran a long time in New York, more than two years. Suddenly it was already 1951; and a whole new rage was blowing in the wind. The anti-communist tempest had begun. You wouldn't be writing such straightforward critical work about America after 1950. Indeed, I don't recall a single play that analyzed American capitalism as severely.

KULLMAN: Even your own?

MILLER: Well, I did *A View from the Bridge*, and that had a side to it that was critical, and of course *The Crucible* was a head-on confrontation but such critiques were diminishing because America, the country, was on the defensive. And part of the defense was aggression. We struck back after being criticized.

KULLMAN: You have a very good relationship with directors and actors, and you are helping the Signature Theater right now with their production of *The American Clock*. Did you have any influence on the actors who have played Willy Loman? Lee J. Cobb? George C. Scott? Dustin Hoffman? Any others?

MILLER: Well, not with George, because he worked completely apart from me and I had no input into that production. I am sorry to say that some of the casting wasn't very good. The Hoffman production I was very intimately involved in, right from the beginning. I thought that the production itself was very strong.

KULLMAN: How bound by the text have various directors been? With Shakespeare's plays so much license is often taken.

MILLER: They haven't yet taken any license. They're waiting for me to die. As far as I am aware, they have been faithful to the text. Now, there was a film of *Salesman* made by a very good director Wim Wenders, a Swede. He eliminated the character of Ben, very foolishly; but he also did some other things that had nothing to do with the text. He made it very Swedish. The characters were very lugubrious. And, of course, I regard the play as having a lot of humor, which you couldn't tell from that performance.

KULLMAN: I was surprised to read that when you wrote half of the play that first night you were laughing a lot of the time and speaking out loud to yourself.

MILLER: So much of what Willy thinks can lead you to laugh.

KULLMAN: And teachers enjoy pointing out the many contradictions in Willy's thinking. Willy says one thing and then ten seconds later he says exactly the opposite. Students find that very amusing, too. It works just as well today as it did then. What about the character of Linda Loman? Today we hear so much about co-dependency, a term that probably wasn't around in 1948. Do you think it applies to her?

MILLER: Well, yes. It takes two to tango. She regards Willy as being very brittle, very easily destroyed; and she's got to prop him up or he'll collapse. In a way it's like someone who is dealing with a sick person. She's trying to keep bad news away from him lest he be destroyed by it.

KULLMAN: Much is made of a comment he makes earlier that he's going to be a partner at the Wagner company. Then Ben asks him to come to Alaska with him, and Linda reminds him of his future at the company; truth or lie, we're not sure. But she keeps him back, at home. She's afraid to be adventuresome herself.

MILLER: At all costs she's got to shield him from the truth. She can insinuate the truth sometimes, but not too obviously. When he says, "You're my foundation and my support," that has a double meaning. She's a kind of co-dependent and heroine at the same time.

KULLMAN: How about the boys, Biff and Happy? Robert Anderson says in *I Never Sang for My Father* something about a relationship not ending in death but continuing on after death in the life of the survivor. Do you think there's a chance that Biff will come to terms with who he is and accept his father for the person he was?

MILLER: I think so, as long as he is no longer threatened by him. Then he could possibly accept him as he was without accepting his values, seeing him as a tragic character, and a loving one too.

KULLMAN: One of the most powerful scenes in the play is the climactic scene in the restaurant. When Happy denies his father, people in the audience sometimes gasp in horror; is there any kind of explanation for his behavior that makes him less a culprit and more of a victim?

MILLER: I don't know if you can explain it. He intends to win and be like his father. The same tragedy awaits Happy. It's going to be repeated in him and probably in his children.

KULLMAN: Willy's friend Charley is always there assisting the Lomans in spite of constant rebuffs by Willy. He knows that Willy is resentful and jealous of him. And yet Charley is always there helping. He loves Willy. How can you explain that?

MILLER: Charley would probably drop him someday. But Willy is exciting. Charley's really very boring. He can sit there quietly for a long time without saying anything, and Willy's mind is always rolling all over the place. And that is a very attractive quality for a man like Charley whose mind goes direct to reality. Willy's personality is a counterpart to Charley's own personality. He often wishes he could be a little like Willy. All those contradictions that he recognizes in Willy—while Charley knows they're destructive and tells Willy, "You'd better grow up"—still there's something lovable in Willy because he is so vulnerable.

KULLMAN: There's that lust for life, the zest, the imagination, the strength of this character that brings life of a strange sort to wherever he is.

MILLER: He's constantly thinking of the garden, of planting seeds. Of course, Charley admires Linda a lot. Part of his motive is to help her. Charley's simply being the guardian. Nobody in that house, in his opinion, can be depended upon to do anything; and they are relying on him even though they don't say so. Willy admits as much in his soliloquy where he says, "Charley's a man of few words, and people respect him." Charley knows that Willy envies him, and that's an ego pleasure. He knows that, in certain moods, Willy would much rather be Charley than himself.

KULLMAN: The minor characters are important enough that none of them can be left out: Miss Forsythe; Stanley, the bartender-waiter; and Bernard. How do you feel about them today?

MILLER: They are exactly where they have to be because the story is very strong and they are firmly embedded in the story. What would you do without the waiter? He has more compassion for Willy at that moment than do the two sons. Each part is embedded in the other part. It's one unit, one articulated unit.

KULLMAN: In 1947 Tennessee Williams's *A Streetcar Named Desire* came out, two years before *Salesman*. In *Timebends* you mention that Williams gave you the power to speak. What was your relationship with Williams, and did he influence *Death of a Salesman?*

MILLER: Yes. Tennessee's early plays were very realistic plays, very social. They were almost class-conscious plays. Not much is made of this, quite rightly, as they're not too interesting. So he had to struggle to find his own speech, and I had a parallel struggle. Most of the plays I wrote before *All My Sons* were rather expressionistic. They were not what you would call conventional realism. *All My Sons* was kind of a sport for me. It was a dollarly attempt to write a play that was acceptable. Both of us were unacceptable to the Broadway producer. *The Glass Menagerie* was not a conventional Broadway production. It came out of left field. It was unique at that time. The poetry was appealing. Our theater was bound by conventional realism. You could hardly tell who wrote any play. There were various attempts to break out of this situation. Maxwell Anderson tried to write in iambic pentameter and ended up with some museum pieces. Elmer Rice, way back in the early twenties, was writing *Mr. Zero*, an experimentally expressionistic work. Eugene O'Neill was fiddling with all kinds of forms to break out of the realistic tradition. This struggle, of course, goes back at least a hundred years in Europe—a whole school of them in France especially were writing very pedestrian language. It's the Irish who exploded things with J. M. Synge, who recognized that the main struggle at the turn of the century was to find a way to break the grip of street realism and to reintroduce the imagery of poets. A number of people, myself included, and obviously Tennessee, were struggling with this dilemma of how to hold an audience, to make them feel something with language that was not exactly familiar.

The first achievement of Tennessee's, one which really made a full step forward, was *Menagerie* rather than *Streetcar. Streetcar* was flashier, sexier, and more commercially successful because its story was more available to the audience. The fact that he found a unique voice that way was inspiring to me. He was a couple of years older and I felt I could go more in that direction with confidence. I had been fumbling for years to find my voice. I had wanted to write a play without transitions of any kind. There would be the direct thrust of the story from the first minute, each scene would be cut at its earliest moment, and succeeding scenes would begin at the latest possible moment. *Salesman* was built that way, and it had very little to do with Tennessee. What suddenly was encouraging to me was that nobody else could have written *Streetcar*. Here was a piece of writing that belonged to that author and not six others. You could hear a poet's voice in the theater again. I appreciated that.

KULLMAN: I know you didn't have a strong relationship with William Inge, but for a while in the fifties the three of you were winning a good share of the theater awards. Did you have much contact with him?

MILLER: A little bit. He was so depressed as a person that it was very difficult to make any kind of contact with him. I'd see him and chat about this and that, but I got the feeling that he disliked and feared social occasions, at least the times that I met him, maybe four or five times. We never got into anything that was very deep. He just seemed to be fending off contact.

KULLMAN: What about revisions? Tennessee Williams wrote *Battle of Angels* which became *Orpheus Descending* which became *The Fugitive Kind*. For a scholar doing research on Williams, this can be a nightmare. Which text does one use? When you finished *Salesman* in 1949, did you finish it entirely or were there rewrites?

MILLER: I made one change, as I recall. It appears in the restaurant scene during the dialogue between Biff and Willy, where Biff is telling some truths, some half-truths, and some outright lies about his adventures in seeing Oliver. The original text was so complicated that finally Arthur Kennedy turned to me and said, "I can't follow it myself." I said, "Just hang in there, do something else." So, I went home and that night I rewrote it. Simplified it.

KULLMAN: How would you advise young playwrights who are trying to write about relationships between people?

MILLER: Get into another line of work. I don't know if any advice matters. These situations differ. Sometimes it's better for the playwright if he takes good advice, but how do you know what advice is good? Other times, he should stick to his guns. But that's more and more difficult because for the past century the position of the director has come to dominate the theater, whereas before that, at least in most cases, the writer was the dominant figure. It's very tricky. Consider Chekhov; the first performances of *The Sea Gull* were really quite disastrous. Stanislavsky didn't understand the play; he didn't understand that it was a comedy, an ironical play. And he damned near ruined that play forever. Chekhov could have reacted by trying to fix *The Sea Gull* to suit Stanislavsky's idea that it was dark, tragic, and so on. The truth is that the characters in that play are based on real people. This play was full of commentary about people alive at that time, and everyone knew who they were. It was, therefore, somewhat ruthless but also an affectionate play, a very brave attempt. I think at the time the convention was win, lose, or draw, the play is a play and it goes on as written. Ibsen made changes occasionally. He changed the ending of *A Doll's House* in Germany. Nora didn't leave. The Germans wouldn't stand for it. He either did that or he couldn't put the play on. The Germans were his biggest customers. The German theaters were his support. He couldn't live off twelve people coming into the theater in Norway. I don't know that his motives were gross. He was a director too. He started out as a kind of a director.

KULLMAN: Have you ever made such a compromise?

MILLER: Well, I haven't had to, for one reason or another.

KULLMAN: How would you explain your success with directors?

MILLER: I don't like to interfere while the director is working with actors. The reason is purely political. I think that actors ought to feel like there is a certainty in one's being directed. I don't want to break up the director's authority. Otherwise the actor will start to look to me. His allegiance will be divided. That's a bad thing to happen.

KULLMAN: What was it like working with Elia Kazan?

MILLER: He was the best director that we've ever had that I know of. In *Salesman* and *Streetcar*, he was able to direct realistic psychology with an unrealistic surface, and that was his greatest strength during that time.

KULLMAN: Is there anything you would like to say about why people should go to the theater today, or anything about politics and drama?

MILLER: Drama, any theater, is a manifestly, preeminently public art which exists in historical time. It prospers when the evolution of a society has reached a certain point. But we know politics is embedded in every work of significance. I don't understand why people try to separate these two elements. It's all one twine rope. You cannot separate them. I am not a Greek scholar, but I seem to recall that the Greeks referred to people who had no social sense as idiots, meaning the *id* was dominant in their thinking. That's what the word means. The caring for the fate of man, for the fate of their society, that it not evolve into some evil disorder, is implicit in all their great tragedies, or sometimes explicit. *Oedipus* is not only about the death of a father and mother. His disaster comes because there is a blight on his city which is killing people. It's not a soap opera about incest; it's a tragedy about the fate of a community. Hamlet is not just the son of a mother who is fooling around with a man who has murdered her husband. He's the prince of Denmark, and when it is said, "Something is rotten in the state of Denmark," it's to direct attention to the fact this country has to be governed. The politics of America is implicit in the whole of *Salesman*. The Salesman is close to being the universal occupation of contemporary society—not only in America, but everywhere. Everybody is selling and everything is for sale.

FRANK ARDOLINO

Miller's Poetic Use of Demotic English in Death of a Salesman

The level of language of *Death of a Salesman* has long been a subject of critical discussion. Perhaps because Arthur Miller compared his work to ancient Greek tragedy in which poetic or elevated language was a requirement, early critics responded negatively to Miller's demotic English. T. C. Worsley wrote that the play fails in its "attempt to make a poetic approach to everyday life without using poetry ..." (225). Similarly, John Gassner noted that the play "is well written but is not sustained by incandescent or memorable language ..." (232). However, later critics have pointed out that Miller does make use of poetic devices. Arthur K. Oberg commented on his patterned speech, striking images, and artful cliches (73, 74, 77), while Marianne Boruch discussed his use of objects as metaphors. Finally, Lois Gordon described the entire play as a "narrative poem whose overall purpose can be understood only by consideration of its poetic as well as narrative elements" (98–99).

Miller's poetic use of demotic English, the level of language which characters speak and which describes their actions and environment, creates the play's tragic dimension. To achieve the depths of tragedy, Miller expands the ordinarily limited expressive capabilities of demotic English by exploiting the sounds and multiple meanings of simple verbal, visual, and numerical images. Words for ordinary objects, daily activities, geographical places, and

From *Studies in American Jewish Literature* 17 (1998). © 1998 by *Studies in American Jewish Literature*.

conventional relationships also function as puns and homonyms which recall meanings from other contexts and establish new ones. The resulting verbal patterns and images form an interconnected and multileveled network of associated meanings which exist in two temporal perspectives: chronological time and construct in which meaning echo and mirror each other, creating nightmarish repetition and a sense of stasis. The network of demotic language, which generates these two perspectives, forms an image of Willy's demented psyche and tragic fate. Giles Mitchell points out that Willy suffers from a personality disorder, pathological narcissism, which demands "grandiosity, omnipotence and perfection" (391) rather than normal achievement. Willy's madness is like a fatal flaw, which blinds him to his reality and fills him with arrogance or hubris so that he challenges the limits of his humanity. Then, like an offended god who punishes hubris, Willy's psyche drives him to suicide which he insanely believes will result in his apotheosis. Members of the audience respond with pity and fear to Willy's fate, for the psyche, which is ultimately incomprehensible, is a reality in their own lives and Willy's fate might have been theirs. Moreover, Biff's merciful release from Willy's dreams into normal life does not mitigate this response, for Biff's good fortune underlines the psyche's capriciousness.

1

The play's dominant metaphor is the polyvalent image of time. On the one hand, metaphors for chronological time represent physical reality and normal human development from youth to maturity to old age and from one generation to the next. Linda, Charley, and his son Bernard and Frank Wagner and his son Howard live in harmony with chronological time, a condition which Biff achieves after he experiences a profound psychological change. On the other hand, images of stasis represent personality disorders which afflict Willy, Happy, and Biff.

The play's three-part temporal setting—night, the next day, and the following night—indicates the progression of chronological time. But on another level, the temporal setting is an image of containment and stasis which alludes to the play's primary subject, Willy's imprisonment in neurosis and his consequent death. The nighttime settings, along with Willy's ominous cliches, "I'm tired to the death" (13) and "I slept like a dead one," (71) portend his suicide. Moreover, although the daytime setting during act 2, before Willy goes out for the day, Linda mentions a grace period to him (72). The grace period, the time before their insurance premium is due, also alludes to Willy's beliefs that on this day his employer will give him a non-traveling job and that Biff will get a loan to go into business with Happy. The grace period, however, does not give rise to the fulfillment of Willy's desires, but proves to be a mocking prelude to his death.

Much of the play takes place in a psychological construct which Willy creates. An Eden-like paradise which lies at the center of his neurosis, it is characterized by the paradoxical union of reality and his delusory fulfillment of his grandiose dreams of omnipotence. Willy's paradise is identified with the time in which Biff and Happy were growing up in Brooklyn, when they expressed, reflected, and validated his belief in their virtual divinity. Willy ironically incorporated the human concept of progress and the future, time's movement, into his changeless paradise. He believed that Biff, who was already "divine" as a football player, would become more so as a businessman. However, before Biff realized Willy's projected future, he lost faith in Willy's dreams, left the state of mind or paradise Willy had created, and destroyed its coherence. As a result, Willy moved from the condition of stasis to one characterized by a confusion of the present and his fragmented paradise. Willy never experiences the future which is part of normal chronological time because he recognizes only the hyperbolic future which he believes is latent in his paradise. To his destruction, he seeks to actualize it.

Images which Willy uses to express his beliefs in his and his sons' divine power suggest the opposite, powerlessness, or allude to and echo events which undercut his extravagant claims. Confusing divine omnipotence with his sons' good looks and personalities, Willy compares them to Adonis, and implies that their inherent qualities will make them successful businessmen just as the inherent power of gods allow them to achieve without effort:

> That's why I thank Almighty God you're both built like Adonises.
> Because the man who makes an appearance in the business world,
> the man who creates personal interest, is the man who gets ahead.
> Be liked and you will never want ... (33)

Willy points to himself as an exemplar of his beliefs, using his name as a manifestation of his omnipotence.

> You take me for instance. I never have to wait in line to see a
> buyer.... "Willy Loman is here!" That's all they have to know, and
> I go right through. (33)

Elaborating on name imagery that echoes his own grandiose self-assessment, Willy expresses his belief in Biff's omnipotence and predicts limitless success for his future in business: "And Ben! When he walks into a business office his name will sound out like a bell and all the doors will open to him!" (86). Name imagery, however, also reveals Willy and Biff's failures. In reality, Willy has been working on commission "like a beginner, an unknown" (57). After he overhears Biff tell Linda and Happy that businessmen have laughed at him for years (61), he pathetically asserts his importance by using names:

> They laugh at me, heh? Go to Filene's, go to the Hub, go to Slattery's, Boston. Call out the name Willy Loman and see what happens! Big Shot! (62)

Name imagery also reveals Biff's failure to develop a career. When he attempted to meet with Bill Oliver, a businessman, he waited in Oliver's reception room, and "[k]ept sending [his] name in" (104), but it meant nothing to Oliver, and his door remained closed. Moreover, when announcing a name, ringing a bell, and opening a door constitute the dramatic action, it contrasts Willy's belief in his omnipotence with his base behavior. Upon Biff's arrival at Willy's hotel, he asks the telephone operator to ring his room to announce his arrival; when Biff opens the door to Willy's room, he discovers Willy's adultery.

Willy believes that Biff's success as a high school football player is proof of his divinity. As he talks to Ben about him, he points to Biff who stands silently by them like a divine presence. Biff wears his school sweater, symbolic of his athletic career, carries a suitcase, which alludes to Willy and his job as a traveling salesman and to Biff's projected future as a businessman. Happy, like an attendant to a god, carries Biff's regalia, his shoulder guards, gold helmet, and football pants (86). Willy, who believes that Biff, like his gods, fulfills his adage, "Be liked and you will never want" (33), momentarily turns from Ben to remind Biff of his god-like condition and responsibilities: "And that's why when you get out on that field today it's important. Because thousands of people will be rooting for you and loving you" (86).

This iconic image of Biff, however, also alludes to other incidents which occur in reality and prove Willy's beliefs empty. The suitcase suggests Biff's trip to Boston where he discovers his father's betrayal of him and Linda, and his football uniform, which marks the height of his achievement, also points to his failure to graduate from high school. He dropped out and spent the next seventeen years moving from one marginal job to another.

Football imagery not only separates Biff from Willy, but also connects him with Miss Francis and alludes to Willy's having betrayed him. At the Boston hotel, after Willy attempts to deny his relationship with Miss Francis and tells her to leave his room, she turns to Biff and asks, "Are you football or baseball?" "Football," he replies. "That's me too," she says (119–20).

Gardening and building images are also used to express the madness of Willy's paradisiacal state of mind. Willy points out the bucolic aspects of Brooklyn when it was his paradise:

> This time of year it was lilac and wisteria. And then the peonies would come out, and the daffodils. What fragrance in this room! (17)

Willy continues to use garden imagery to contrast the satisfaction and joy he took in the past when his paradise was intact with the anger he feels toward the urban present when his paradise is fragmented by the increase in traffic and the number of apartment houses (17). As Willy goes on, however, he unwittingly alludes to himself as the destroyer of his garden and of his family in a metaphorical sense: "Remember those two beautiful elm trees out there? ... They should've arrested the builder for cutting those down ..." (17). On one level, the two trees are allusions to the Tree of Life and the Tree of Good and Evil, echoes of Willy's Edenic paradise. On another level, the trees allude to Biff, who uses plant imagery to explain his failure to achieve a career—"I just can't take hold, Mom. I can't take hold of some kind of a life" (54)—and to Happy. The builder whom Willy complains about refers to himself, for he has the skills of a carpenter and rebuilds much of his house: "All the cement, the lumber, the reconstruction I put in this house! There ain't a crack to be found in it any more" (74). Willy's house, however, which is a sound structure as a result of his efforts, is a metaphor for his mind, an air-tight prison which confines him in neurosis. Miller reverses the slang use of the word "crack" as "crazy" to suggest that Willy might have escaped his insanity if his house/mind had had a crack in it to allow help to reach him.

Because of his madness, Willy, who literally rebuilds his house, destroys it in the metaphorical sense of progeny or line of descent.

> LINDA: Well, it [their house] served its purpose.
> WILLY: What purpose? ... If only Biff would take this house, and raise a family.... (74)

Ironically, the metaphorical level of language reveals that Charley, who does not have the skills of a carpenter, has successfully built where Willy has failed. Charley's son Bernard matured in harmony with chronological time. He completed his education, became a lawyer, married and had two children. He met mundane expectations, paradoxically only to exceed them. When

Willy meets Bernard in Charley's office, he is about to leave for Washington, D.C. To argue a case in the highest arena in his profession, the Supreme Court. The word "supreme," which recalls the "S" on Biff's high school sweater (28) and Willy's belief that Biff would become a superman, mocks Willy's deluded hope and recalls that seventeen years earlier Biff played in a championship football game at prestigious Ebbets Field, but did not go on to a career of any kind. "His life ended after that Ebbets Field game," confides Willy to Bernard (92). He "laid down and died like a hammer hit him!" (93). Ironically, Willy's reference to a hammer, a tool used to build, points to the fact that he, himself, is Biff's destroyer. The image of the hammer mocks Willy who failed as a father by echoing the insulting statement he made to Charley: "A man who can't handle tools is not a man. You're disgusting" (44). It also mocks Biff's failure to become a professional athlete and alludes to Charley and Bernard's professional success: "Great athlete! Between him and his son Bernard they can't hammer a nail! (51)," says Willy contemptuously. Willy's hammering in his garden at night, a negative image of creation, mirrors his tragic reversal of life and death—his belief that he will achieve the future which his neurosis demands by committing suicide.

Like Willy's garden, his Chevy symbolizes his paradise and the particular satisfaction he takes in the mutually reflective relationship he has with his sons. He associates the Chevy with the abundance of nature: "But it's so beautiful up there, Linda, the trees are so thick, and the sun is warm. I opened the windshield [of the Chevy] and just let the warm air bathe over me" (14). The care his son bestowed upon the Chevy represents their past admiration for each other: "Ts. Remember those days? The way Biff used to simonize that car? The dealer refused to believe there was eighty thousand miles on it" (19). "Simonizing" or "waxing," a pun on Willy's waxing euphoric, alludes to the fullness of emotion he experienced in their relationship.

The Chevy, however, is also associated with the personal and professional failures that the Lomans experience in reality. The car is connected through numbers with the great football career Willy believed that Biff would have as a result of his playing quarterback in a championship game at Ebbets field. In response to his friend Charley's skepticism, Willy yells, "Touchdown! Touchdown! Eighty-thousand people!" ... (90), echoing the eighty thousand miles on the car. And when Willy tried to convince Howard to give him a non-traveling job, Willy recalls the year 1928, the model of the Chevy, as the height of his professional success and acceptance in the business world: "[I]n 1928 I had a big year ... (82)."

Images of geographical expansiveness further reflect Willy's emotional inflation and the inevitable collapse that results from it. In his description of a business trip, Willy evokes and identifies with the grandeur of New England and its history. However, the names of the cities along his route, which is a metaphor for the downward course of his life, are not only images of aggrandizement but of pain that Willy and Biff suffer after their inflated emotions collapse. Providence, the name of Willy's first stop, is presided over by a mayor whose title suggests an eponymous deity. Rather than providing Willy with care and benevolent guidance, however, the mayor of Providence confers a malign fate on him, as the names of the other places on his route attest. "Waterbury, a big clock city" (31), is an image of time which mocks the Loman's and their dreams of success. Moreover, it is also an allusion to Willy's attempt to commit suicide by driving his car into a river (59). Willy's praise of "Boston, the cradle of the Revolution" (31), presages Biff's disillusionment with Willy from him after finding him in a Boston hotel in an adulterous relationship. Portland is the city Willy is unable to reach because of his mental breakdown. Metaphorically, Portland suggests Willy's failure to achieve "port" or fulfillment that he might have expected during the last years of his career. Along with the word "boat," "Portland" alludes to Willy's insane conviction that his dreams will become reality through suicide. Linda, who pities Willy and understands him as a man who has failings, but not as a neurotic, asks Biff to be "sweet" and "loving" to him "[b]ecause he's only a little boat looking for a harbor" (76). The image becomes horrific just prior to his suicide when he psychologically joins Ben, who acts as a Charon figure to bring him to port in the land of the dead.

> BEN: Time, William, Time! ... (*Looking at his watch*) The boat. We'll be late. (*He moves slowly off into the darkness.*) (135)

Bangor, the name of the last city on Willy's route, onomatopoetically explodes—"bang!"—echoing imagery of emotional inflation and collapse associated with Willy's paradisiacal past. Years after Biff became disillusioned with Willy, he uses imagery of inflation to blame Willy for his failure to achieve a career: "... I never got anywhere because you [Willy] blew me so full of hot air I could never stand taking orders from anybody" (131). And he accuses Happy of being a liar: "You big blow, are you the assistant buyer? You're one of the two assistants to the assistant, aren't you?" (131). The group of three which Biff describes forms a deflated parallel to the one Willy once imagined would create a sensation upon entering the Boston stores— Biff and Happy accompanying him, carrying his sample bags: "Oh, won't that be something! Me comin' into the Boston stores with you boys carryin' my bags" (31). In the light of the Lomans' lack of success, the bags, suggestive of wind-bags, reflect, finally, the burden of Willy's meretricious beliefs and the unfounded grandiosity that Biff and Happy bore.

Ultimately, images of inflated emotion and collapse cruelly come together in the word "blow," meaning "to treat" as well as "a violent impact," and in the name of the restaurant, "Frank's Chop House." The name "Frank" recalls Frank Wagner, who has been replaced by his heartless son, and "chop", which literally refers to a cut of meat, also means "a sharp blow." In anticipation of getting a loan to establish a sporting goods business, Biff asks Linda to invite Willy to a celebration at Frank's Chop House: "Tell Dad, we want to blow him to a big meal" (74).

Willy expects to make the dinner a dual triumph. He feels sure that his current employer, Howard Wagner, will give him the non-traveling job that he wants. That evening, however, when the three Lomans meet, Willy announces that Howard fired him, and Biff reluctantly tells Willy that Bill Oliver did not give him the loan. When Biff orders drinks that evening, "Scotch all around. Make it doubles" (105), he unwittingly signifies their dual failures.

2

Hidden in Willy's images of a past paradise is an Eve-like temptress, a personification of his neurosis. This ambiguous character, who is a siren on one level and Miss Francis, the woman with whom Willy commits adultery on another, stands in opposition to Linda who is associated with the diurnal rhythms of chronological time and mundane reality. The strength of Willy and Biff's disordered relationship is tested and broken when Willy introduces Miss Francis to him at the Boston hotel. Willy's adultery is obvious, but Willy wants Biff to deny what he sees and understands:

> [N]ow listen pal, she's just a buyer.... Now stop crying and do as
> I say. I gave you an order. Biff, I gave you an order! (120)

Biff, however, does not comply. Seventeen years later, the word "order" echoes Willy's loss of power over Biff in a conversation in which Willy and Bernard talk about Biff's failure to make up a high school math course.

> BERNARD: Did you tell him [Biff] not to go to summer school?
> WILLY: Me? I begged him to go. I ordered him to go! (93)

Mathematics, a metaphor for order in mundane reality, and Mr. Birnbaum, its personification, also reveal the damage that Willy does by taking over Biff's life and preventing him from maturing in chronological time. Biff's age, seventeen, and the four points by which he fails math echo and contrast with Ben's achievement. Ben, Willy's dead brother and his image of an ideal business man, was seventeen when he set out to make his fortune. Four years later, he was rich (48). The repetition of "seventeen" and "four" also contrasts Biff's stasis with Bernard's progress in chronological time. Seventeen years after Biff failed math at the age of seventeen, he has no career, but Bernard has become a lawyer. When Willy congratulates him on his success, he alludes to Biff's failure: "I'm—I'm overjoyed to see how you made the grade, Bernard, overjoyed" (92).

Mathematics and Mr. Birnbaum reveal the meretriciousness of Willy's dream. Mr. Birnbaum rejects Willy's conviction that personal attractiveness is more important that actual achievement and refuses to give Biff the four points he needed to pass, thus motivating his trip to Boston. Birnbaum's name comments on the consequences of the trip for both Biff and Willy. As Karl Harshbarger noted, the first syllable in "Birnbaum" is reminiscent of fire and the second one means "tree" in German (58). The whole name echoes Willy's cry of disaster, "the woods are burning" (41, 107). Willy uses the phrase to signify trouble just before he tells Biff and Happy that he was fired. In the circumstances, it is a double pun. At the hotel, Willy, who knows that Biff is knocking on the door of his room, refuses to open it, but The Woman insists: "Maybe the hotel's on fire!" (116). Her exclamation echoes Willy's locution and alludes to imminent disaster for him—Biff's recognition of his duplicity.

After Biff tells Willy why he came to the hotel, he imitates Mr. Birnbaum as he did for his classmates at school:

> ... I got up at the blackboard and imitated him. I crossed my eyes and talked with a lithp.... The thquare root of thixthy twee is ... (118)

Biff's crossed eyes, which parody Mr. Birnbaum's eyes, are part of a palimpsest of related images and concepts. Without Biff's realizing it, his eyes allude to the remark that The Woman made to Willy just before his arrival: "You are the saddest, self-centerest soul I ever did see-saw ..." (116). The word "see-saw" presages Biff's seeing and realizing Willy's having betrayed him and Linda. "See-saw," which joins past and present tenses of "to see," also alludes to Willy's disordered experience of time after Biff breaks the bond of their relationship. Moreover, as the image of a child's toy, a see-saw mockingly contrasts Willy's actual position with his dream of divine success. Contrary to ordinary expectations, Willy holds the same job at the end of his career as he did at the beginning of it—working on commission. The movement of the see-saw—its ups and downs in place—contrasts Howard Wagner's rise in the business world with Willy's stasis. At the age of 36, the transposition of Willy's age and the number of years that Willy worked for the Wagners (56), Howard is the head of the company and Willy's superior. Finally, Howard's position contrasts his father Frank's success with Willy's failure. Frank passed on his company to Howard, but Willy has nothing to give his sons.

The math problem, the "thquare root of thixthy twee," is a coded message which reveals Willy's insanity and Biff's participation in it, but they do not recognize its significance. The number "63," Willy's age, identifies him as the focus of the problem. The word "square," an image of an enclosed area, and "root," a plant image, refer to Willy's paradisiacal garden, the two trees representing Biff and Happy which grew there, and the condition of his mind which is imprisoned in insanity, the root of his and his family's problem. Ironically, when Biff concludes his imitation by saying that Birnbaum walked in, drawn by Willy and Biff's laughter, The Woman, whose entrance parallels Mr. Birnbaum's, leaves the bathroom, her hiding place, and enters Willy's room. Biff's eyes are no longer "crossed" and he finally sees who Willy is.

Stocking imagery further unites Willy, The Woman/Miss Francis, and Linda and Biff in a cycle of betrayal and its recognition. Stockings refer to the nylons Willy gives to Miss Francis, the stock that he sells as a salesman, his status with Biff, and the Loman familial line. During one of Willy's hallucinations, Linda "darns stockings" (36) prior to The Woman's appearance and "mends a pair of her silk stockings" (39) just after her disappearance. When Willy sees Linda at her work, his reaction is intense, for her stockings recall his adultery: "I won't have you mending stockings in this house! Now throw them out!" (39). Willy gives stockings to The Woman in exchange for her favors. "And thanks for the stockings," she says to him. "I love a lot of stockings" (39). When Biff surprises Willy and The Woman in his hotel room, she insists on her gift even while Willy desperately tries to get rid of her: "You had two boxes of size nine sheers for me, and I want them!" (119). Betrayers and the betrayed come together in a "stocking" image when Biff poignantly recognizes Willy's adultery and rejects him: "You—you gave her Mama's stockings!" (121).

"Sheers," the word that Miss Francis uses to refer to silk stockings, also is a pun for "scissors" and suggests cutting, which in turn alludes to Biff's metaphorically cutting the tie that has bound him to Willy. After Biff arrives at home, he burns his sneakers on which he had printed "University of Virginia" (33–34), an act which echoes Willy's utterance of disaster. The act also alludes to the story of Adam and Eve's expulsion from the Garden of Eden for it symbolizes Biff's change from innocence to knowledge, his rejection of Willy's beliefs, and his departure from Willy's paradise. Seventeen years later, at Frank's Chop House, Biff "takes the rolled up hose from his pocket ..." (115) and shows it to Happy. Another synonym for stocking, the hose is the means by which Willy planned to commit suicide.

Biff's attempt to get the loan from Oliver has not resulted in the recreation of the Lomans' mutually reflective relationship, but in Biff's freedom from Willy's domination and movement to psychological health. Earlier images which Willy used to express his vision of Biff's omnipotence—his name's sounding like a bell and opening all doors to him (86)—are echoed in Biff's unwilled insight and ironically compare the experience to the mysteriousness of divine intervention. After Oliver refuses to talk with him, Biff psychologically awakens as if he hears the sound of a bell. For no explainable reason, Biff suddenly realizes the value of his ordinary human life and accepts his identity or name which opens the door to the possibility of his living normally in chronological time.

As a result of Biff's revelation, he and Willy engage in an agon at the Chop House. Biff tries to make Willy see and accept him as an individual, but Willy struggles to return Biff to his former identity as his alter ego. At this point, Willy vacillates between reality and the hallucination of the past when Biff knocked at the door of Willy's hotel room in Boston. In reality, at the restaurant Biff makes a joke of the blow Willy dealt him and offers him acceptance and forgiveness, an act which would have been impossible for him before his revelation. However, Willy, who is about to accept Biff's invitation, turns away from him and responds to The Woman, who pulls him back into the hallucination and asks him to open the hotel room door. An image of guilt and forgiveness, imprisonment and release, the door suggests Willy's betrayal of Linda and Biff and Biff's psychological release from him and his forgiving him. The washroom in Frank's Chop House, which is conflated with the bathroom where The Woman hid, also evokes Linda's washing clothes (33, 47, 85) and her forgiving Willy.

However, Linda's selfless devotion and Biff's filial love are not strong enough to free Willy from his neurosis. Willy does not relinquish his insane dream even after Biff begs him to give it up. Willy imagines that his death will be the means of his and Biff's long-awaited apotheosis as business gods like Ben and Dave Singleman.

Willy's last utterances refer or allude to images of his and Biff's deification and to his own insanity. With great enthusiasm, he asks Ben, "Can you imagine that magnificence [Biff] with twenty thousand dollars in his pocket?" (135). Willy's reference to his life insurance policy echoes Charley's description of J. P. Morgan: "Why must everybody like you? Who liked J. P. Morgan? Was he impressive? In a Turkish bath he'd look like a butcher. But with his pockets on he was very well-liked" (97). Willy carries out his plan to literally put money into Biff's pockets in the demented belief that he will become the equivalent of his gods, businessmen like J. P. Morgan.

Willy completes his vision of the future by translating Biff's love to worship, thus achieving divinity like Dave's in Biff's eyes, and by identifying with Biff whom he believes will become as successful as Ben: "[H]e'll worship me for it!.... Oh Ben, I always knew one way or another we were gonna make it, Biff and I!" (135). Finally, Willy sees himself as becoming the embodiment of all success and all time—the eternal in death and the dynamic with Biff in life.

In summary, the imagery which we have discussed, while not exhaustive, exemplifies Miller's poetic use of demotic language. Through his system of associated meanings and dual temporal schemes, Miller infuses the commonplace with tragic significance which mirrors Willy's madness and fate.

WORKS CITED

Boruch, Marianne. "Miller and Things." *Literary Review* 24.4 (1981): 548–61.

Gassner, John. "*Death of a Salesman*: First Impressions, 1949." In Weales. 231–39.

Gordon, Lois. "*Death of a Salesman*: An Appreciation." In Koon. 98–108.

Harshbarger, Karl. *The Burning Jungle: An Analysis of Arthur Miller's Death of a Salesman.* Washington, D.C.: University Press of America, 1979.

Koon, Helene, ed. *Twentieth Century Interpretations of Death of a Salesman.* Princeton, New Jersey: Princeton University Press, 1983.

Miller, Arthur. *Death of a Salesman: Certain Private Conversations in Two Acts and a Requiem.* New York: Penguin, 1949.

Mitchell, Giles. "Living and Dying for the Ideal: A Study of Willy Loman's Narcissism." *The Psychoanalytic Review* 77:3 (Fall 1990): 391–407.

Oberg, Arthur. "*Death of a Salesman* and Arthur Miller's Search for Style." In Weales. 70–78.

Weales, Gerald, ed. *Death of a Salesman: Text and Criticism.* New York: Penguin Books, 1967.

Worsley, T. C. "Poetry Without Words." In Weales. 224–27.

TERRY OTTEN

Death of a Salesman *at Fifty—*
Still "Coming Home to Roost"

"Tragedy," Eric Bentley has warned, can "easily lure us into talking nonsense" (*Playwright*, 128). If so, *Death of a Salesman* surely doubles the risk. For likely no modern drama has generated more such talk than Miller's classic American play. After only two decades of strenuous debate seemed to have exhausted the subject, critics began to complain about "the pointless academic quibbles" about whether or not *Death of a Salesman* is a "true" tragedy (Weales, *American Drama*, 3). Such topics, wrote Lois Gordon in 1969, "have been explored ad nauseum" (98). Yet thirty years later and a half-century after the play's premiere, the question of its fitness as a tragedy continues to be a central critical concern.

Of course, Miller himself provided much of the impetus for the critical battles by writing his controversial 1949 essay on "Tragedy and the Common Man" in defense of Willy Loman as a suitable subject for tragedy, an essay later the same year on "The Nature of Tragedy," and a number of important essays in subsequent years, including the preface "On Social Plays" published in the 1955 one-act edition of *A View from the Bridge* and *A Memory of Two Mondays*. Furthermore, the issue was and still is raised one way or the other in many, if not most, interviews, often by Miller himself. Although he admitted in the 1957 introduction to the Collected Plays that "I set out not 'to write a tragedy'" and called *Death of a Salesman* "a slippery play" to

From *Texas Studies in Literature and Language* 41, no. 3 (Fall 1999): 280–307. Later collected in *The Temptation of Innocence in the Dramas of Arthur Mille*r © 2002 by the Curators of the University of Missouri.

categorize, he defended it against "some of the attacks upon it as a pseudo-tragedy" (*Theater Essays*, 144): "I need not claim that this is a genuine solid-gold tragedy for my opinions on tragedy to be held valid" (146).[1]

By the time he wrote the foreword to his *Theater Essays* (first edited by Robert A. Martin in 1977), Miller admitted, "I have often wished I had never written a word on the subject of tragedy" (*Theater Essays*, lv), and then, "[t]he damage having been done," he went on to argue for the validity of modern tragedy, concluding, "I have not yet seen a convincing explanation of why the tragic mode seems anachronistic now, nor am I about to attempt one" (lv).

The controversy, however, has never really abated among critics, and the topic inevitably continues to surface in interviews. By the time Matthew Roudané interviewed him in November of 1983, Miller seemed less defensive and insistent. Responding to the question of whether or not *Death of a Salesman* was a Sophoclean tragedy, he commented, "I think it does engender tragic feelings, at least in a lot of people. Let's say it's one kind of tragedy. I'm not particularly eager to call it tragedy or anything else; the label doesn't matter to me" (*Conversations*, 361). And in a recent interview in 1997 he claimed that when people ask him what the play is about, he simply responds, "Well, it's about a salesman and he dies. What can I tell you?" (Mandell).[2]

But undeniably the "damage" *has* been done—one way or the other *Death of a Salesman* still provokes critical wars about the viability of tragedy in the modern age, and particularly in American culture. Even as Miller seems to have moved more into the contemporary literary world in his recent dramas and as more critics have begun to see his canon in postmodern terms alien to the concept of tragedy and traditional approaches to the genre, the question still remains dominant in evaluations of a work that Eugene O'Neill may well have prophesied in response to those who argued that tragedy is foreign to the American experience:

> Supposing someday we should suddenly see with the clear eyes of the soul the true valuation of all our triumphant, brass band materialism, see the cost—and the result in terms of eternal values? What a colossal, ironic, 100 percent American tragedy that would be, what? Tragedy not native to our soil? Why we are tragedy the most appalling yet written or unwritten. (*Selected Letters*, 159)

Miller has always admitted his predilection for tragedy, at times at the cost of obfuscating his plays by defending them as tragedies. The plays "that have lasted," he has insisted, "have shared a kind of tragic vision of man"

(*Conversations*, 294). Although "tragedy is still basically the same" and can be traced back to the Bible and "the earliest Western literature, like Greek drama," he told Robert Martin in the late 1960s, "it is unlikely, to say the least, that since so many other kinds of human consciousness have changed that [tragedy] would remain unchanged" (*Conversations*, 200). He acknowledged to Steven Centola in a 1990s interview that his own later plays "may seem more tragic" than his earlier efforts in which "the characters' inability to face themselves gives rise to tragic consequences" ("Just Looking," 86–87). This awareness of an evolving form may partly explain why even those critics who share Miller's belief in the "tragic nature" of *Death of a Salesman* often stop short of declaring it (or other of his plays) an unequivocal or conventional tragedy. They instead allude to its "tragic situations," its evocation of "tragic feelings," its "tragic implications" or "tragic rhythms," or other subthemes of the genre.

Nonetheless, Miller has long confessed that classical tragedy and Ibsen's subsequent adaptation of it in the post-Enlightenment period have provided the structural and thematic spine of his work. Looking back over his career in the mid-1980s, he remarked: "I think probably the greatest single discovery I made was the structure of the Greek plays. That really blinded me. It seemed to fit everything that I felt. And then there was Ibsen, who was dealing with the same kind of structural pattern—that is the past meeting the present dilemma" (*Conversations*, 386).[3] He recalled that as an undergraduate he read "by chance ... a Greek tragedy and Ibsen at the same time" and discovered that "something happened x years ago, unbeknownst to the hero, and he's got to grapple with it" (Bigsby, *Arthur Miller*, 49). His devotion to the tragic mode as he perceives it and his varied experiments with tragic form and matter have made him the more vulnerable to critics bent on showing the deficiencies of his works as tragedies or his mere mimicking of an obsolete literary tradition.

Christopher Bigsby may be right in claiming that "the argument over the tragic status of *Death of a Salesman*, finally, is beside the point" ("Introduction," xviii),[4] but of all Miller plays *Death of a Salesman* has been the lightening rod that has most attracted the unending debates on Miller and tragedy, and any assessment of its endurance and significance after fifty years must engage the question.[5] Most often paralleled with Oedipus, *Death of a Salesman* has also been compared with Shakespearean tragedies (especially *Lear* and *Othello*), Lillo's *The London Merchant*, and various plays by Ibsen, O'Neill, Williams, and others.[6] Attacks on the play as tragedy have ranged from casual dismissal to vitriolic antagonism. Representative views include Eleanor Clark's early severe condemnation of the play's "pseudo-universality" and "party-line" polemics in her 1949 *Partisan Review* essay.

Calling Miller's concept of tragedy "not feasible," Alvin Whitley, among other later critics, admonished Miller to realize "that he is extending the traditional interpretation [of tragedy] to embrace demonstrably different emotional effects" and that "in the basic matter of personal dignity, Willy Loman may have ended where *Hamlet* unquestionably began" (262). Richard J. Foster labeled Willy a "pathetic bourgeois barbarian" and concluded that the drama was "not a 'tragedy' or great piece of literature" (87–88). Reflecting a common theme among Miller critics, Eric Mottram assaulted Miller's "muddled notions of Greek tragedy and modern psychology" which "lead him to plumb for that old stand-by for the American liberal, 'the individual'" (32). For a more recent indication of dismissive critical commentary regarding Miller's sense of tragedy, one might cite Harold Bloom's rather patronizing remark in his 1991 anthology *Willy Loman*: "All that Loman actually shares with Lear and Oedipus is aging; there is no other likeness whatsoever. Miller has little understanding of Classical or Shakespearean tragedy; he stems entirely from Ibsen" (1).

Because no single concept of modern tragedy has ever attained the status of being the standard measure of the genre like Aristotle's *Poetics* in reference to classical tragedy, *Death of a Salesman* is subject to as many interpretations and evaluations as there are definitions. Most modern theories of tragedy severely modify Aristotle whether applied to *Death of a Salesman* or any other modern drama,[7] but certain elemental subthemes have constituted the targets of critics, among them the loss of community and divine order, the victimization and diminution of the hero, the banality of language, the absence of choice, the protagonist's lack of awareness or epiphany, the irresolution of the ending, and the failure to effect a "catharsis."

Perhaps the most sustained historical study of the development of tragedy generally is Robert Heilman's two-volume exploration of the genre, *Melodrama and Tragedy: Versions of Experience* and *The Iceman, The Arsonist, and The Troubled Agent: Tragedy and Melodrama on the Modern Stage*. Distinguishing between tragedies and what he calls "disaster" plays or serious melodrama, Heilman incorporates the thinking of many theorists, proposing that tragedy includes a "divided" hero driven by counter "imperatives" or "impulses," who chooses between irreconcilable opposites, gains awareness, accepts consequences, and evokes emotions of both defeat and victory (what Heilman calls a "polypathic" rather than "monopathic" response). He differentiates between such plays and "disaster" dramas in which characters are mere victims whose deaths shed little or no light on the nature of human experience. Like all such formulaic criticism, Heilman's at times creates a Procrustean bed of criticism in which some plays of dubious merit are raised in stature as "tragic," and superior dramas receive the more pejorative label of "melodrama." Nonetheless, because his study, in addition to offering a useful survey of dramatic theory and major plays, provides a functional definition that allows for critical discriminations to be made, I shall occasionally use his critical terminology, while keeping in mind Bernard Shaw's admonishment that critics can "become so accustomed to formula that at last they cannot relish or understand a play that has grown naturally, just as they cannot admire the Venus of Milo because she has neither corset nor high-heeled shoes" (54). To be sure, different critics using the very same elements cited by Heilman and others have vociferously declared *Death of a Salesman* both "the great American tragedy," and an exemplum of cheap pathos.[8] In response to the play's fiftieth anniversary and continued prominence as what many still conssider "the great American targedy," it seems appropriate to look once more at the issues raised in the critical debate as they have been amplified and qualified by different theoretical approaches.

Underlying any consideration of the play's tragic potential is the larger question of whether or not tragedy can exist in an age when "God is dead." Nietzsche warned that it would go hard with tragic poets if God is dead, and writers like Joseph Wood Krutch and George Steiner have long since pronounced the death of tragedy, largely on the grounds that the absence of some identifiable, universal moral law that locates the operation of a transcendent order against which to judge the tragic hero denies the possibility of tragic drama. Miller himself has certainly recognized the problem this poses. When asked if his plays were "modern tragedies," he admitted,

> I changed my mind about it several times.... To make direct and arithmetical comparison between any contemporary work and the classic tragedies is impossible because of the function of religion and power, which was taken for granted in an *a priori* consideration of any classic tragedy. (*Conversations*, 88)

In a seminal discussion on the nature of tragedy with Robert Corrigan, Miller identified society as

> the only thing we've got in modern times that has any parallel to the ancient deities .... [A]nd what it lacks is sublimity because at bottom, I think, most people ... have no sense of divinity ... and this is what cuts down the tragic vision. It levels.

And he went on to explain, "By society, I don't mean, of course, merely the government. It is the whole way we live, what we want from life and what we do to get it" (*Conversations*, 254). In the same interview he noted that the classic hero

> is working inside a religious cosmology where there is no mistaking a man for God; he is conscious to begin with that he is in the hands of God.... We are in the middle of a scrambled egg and mucking about in it, and the difference between the points of contact with the man and his god, so to speak, are fused. (255)

In effect, in a secular universe the moral center shifts to the individual in relationship to his social environment. As Miller told Robert Martin, "What we've got left is the human half of the old Greek and the old Elizabethan process" in which human beings were measured against the presence of the gods (*Conversations*, 202). As a consequence, Miller concluded,

> if we're going to talk about tragedy at all ... we've got to find some equivalent to the superhuman schema that had its names in the past, whatever they were. Whether they went under the name of Zeus's laws, or, as in Shakespearean times, reflected a different ideology toward man, they also had lying in the background somewhere an order which was being violated and which the character was seeking to come to some arrangement with. (*Conversations*, 201)

In *Death of a Salesman* society assumes the role of the gods to whom Willy gives allegiance. It constitutes what Heilman calls an "imperative," an obligation to a given, externally located code that compels the tragic hero to act in direct opposition to an opposing imperative or "impulse," which Heilman characterizes as a personal or egocentric need or desire. The dilemma is underscored with irony, though, because unlike the traditional gods of tragedy, Willy's gods prove to be morally indifferent. As Rita Di Giuseppe has written, they have "metamorphosed ... into the fat gods of consumerism" (115). Miller's depiction of such a secular universe has inevitably led to the protesting cry of some critics who apparently want Miller to provide a transcendent moral force that would belie the realism of his conception.[9] He often frustrates them by contextualizing the play in a realistic, if expressionistic, form that seems too reductive to allow for the grandeur of tragedy; but he encloses within this realism a tragic rhythm that depends upon the integrity of his uncompromised realism. The "discovery of the moral law," he wrote in "Tragedy and the Common Man," is no longer "the discovery of some abstract or metaphysical quantity" but is grounded in the nature of human experience itself (*Theater Essays*, 5).

Eric Bentley offered the much repeated view in his *In Search of Theater* that *Death of a Salesman* futilely attempts to align tragedy with social drama, the one conceiving of the hero as responsible for his own fate and the other as the pathetic victim of a severely flawed society.[10] But, as Christopher Bigsby has observed, surely *Oedipus* and *Hamlet* integrate social drama and tragedy ("Introduction," xviii). For Miller, "there are certain duties and social fears that can create a tragic event," specifically when the dialectic develops "between the individual and his social obligations, his social self" (*Conversations*, 346). Miller has described Greek tragedies as "social documents, not little piddling private conversations" written by "a man confronting his society" (*Conversations*, 101). The differences that emerge in modern tragedy when realistically described social forces usurp the role of the gods transfigure tragedy profoundly—but not unrecognizably. Miller has called what emerges "the tragedy of displacement," in which "the tragic dimension" surfaces in the protagonist's struggle for a lost "personal identity" displaced by "the social mask" (*Conversations*, 347). In "Tragedy and the Common Man" he attributed "the terror and fear that is classically associated with tragedy" to the "inner dynamic" driven by the "total onslaught of the individual against the seemingly stable cosmos surrounding us" (*Theater Essays*, 4). Not unlike in *Hamlet*, though obviously different from it, the tragic conflict pits one imperative against another: the social imperative of success in direct competition with the personal imperative or "impulse" of finding the authentic self. This transformation of the tragic conflict generates concomitant tensions in the form and focus of the text, between the outer and inner worlds, between Willy as hero and Willy as a psychological case study, between social commentary and personal experience, between the socially accepted view of morality and personal guilt, between suicide and self-sacrifice—in short, between melodramatic documentary and modern tragedy.

Miller himself has sensed the precarious nature of his plays as tragedy, admitting in his essay "On Social Plays" that "The debilitation of the tragic drama ... is commensurate with the fracturing and the aborting of the need of man to maintain a fruitful kind of union with his society" (*Theater Essays*, 62). Furthermore, he has implied that his artistic end in *Death of a Salesman* was closer to Ibsen than to Sophocles. In *Timebends* he confessed that he "wanted to set off before the captains and the so seemingly confident kings the corpse of a believer," to plant "a time bomb under American capitalism" (184); but he knew this differed from the Greek plays which, at the end, "return to confirm the rightness of the laws" (*Theater Essays*, 6). His purpose was political and satirical, for he knew, as Christopher Bigsby has written, that "Willy Loman's American dream is drained of transcendence. It is faith in the supremacy of the material over the spiritual" ("Introduction," xxiii). It is little wonder that Miller threatened a lawsuit when he was asked to permit a twenty-five minute short to be shown before the film version of the play to assure the audience that "nowadays selling was a fine profession with limitless spiritual compensations as well as financial ones"—indeed, it *would* have made the play "*morally* meaningless, a tale told by an idiot signifying nothing" (*Timebends*, 315).

Because Miller both creates a naturalistic, almost Marxist view of American culture in the post-Depression era, some have reduced the drama to social determinism. And the truth is Miller *does* describe Willy as a childlike victim of the cultural values he adopts virtually without question. In Miller's words, he "carried in his pocket the coinage of our day" (*Conversations*, 176) as a "true believer" in the American dream of success. The very embodiment of the myth, he carried an unidentified "product" in his case, "the cipher," in Stephen Barker's reading, "of an empty signifier" (88). And yet Miller grants Willy stature and significance because of, as much as despite, his dogged commitment to a pernicious ideal. One cannot take away Willy's dream without diminishing him, Miller has suggested: "[T]he less capable a man is of walking away from the central conflict of the play, the closer he approaches a tragic existence" (*Theater Essays*, 118). Ironically, like Oedipus, who at every point insists on fulfilling his obligation as king by unwittingly searching for his own father's murderer even though it finally destroys him to do so, Willy unreservedly follows his imperative to its fatal end, similarly encouraged by all the others around him to abort his quest: Linda, Biff and Happy, Charley, and Bernard all urge him to give up, just as Teiresias, the Chorus, Jocasta, and the shepherd plead with Oedipus to do the same. That Willy does not finally understand the corruptness of the dream exposes his intellectual failure, but he dies in defense of the imperative that consumes him. When in a symposium on the play John Beaufort and David W. Thompson argued that Willy "has no moral values at all," Miller contended that "The trouble with Willy Loman is that he has tremendously powerful ideals.... The fact is that he has values" (*Conversations*, 30). As he told the Chinese actors for the 1983 production in Beijing, Willy "hasn't a cynical bone in his body, he is a walking believer, the bearer of a flame.... He is forever signaling to a future that he cannot describe and will not live to see, but he is in love with it all the same" (*Salesman*, 49). Even though the imperative devastates him as it does Oedipus, and even though it ironically proves false, Willy "in his fumbling and often ridiculous way ... is trying to lift up a belief in immense redeeming human possibilities" (49).[11] What matters finally is not so much the validity of the ideal but that Willy offers himself up to affirm it. It motivates him just as the oracle compels Oedipus to fulfill his kingship. However ironically, Willy fulfills his role as salesman with the same determination that compels Oedipus to affirm his kingship.

But it would be absurd to argue Willy's tragic stature on the grounds of his innocent, misguided commitment to the American dream of success, even though his devotion to the code is no less consuming than Oedipus's or Hamlet's commitment to their imperatives. At a deeper level we must ask *why* he invests so totally and self-destructively in support of the dream. For Oedipus or Hamlet, of course, the moral imperative was a given—there was divine order, after all, a divinity that shapes human destiny. For Willy, however, the imperative was not so readily apparent or universally acclaimed. His fierce devotion to it was not for its own sake, but rather it was for Willy a means to an end. In a critically important comment, Miller contended that "Willy is demanding of the market and of his job some real return *psychically*" (*Conversations*, 297–98, emphasis mine). He seeks self-dignity and with it something more, what most defines the counter to the social imperative in the play, to recover the lost love of Biff and preserve the family. Willy does not want simply to fulfill the imperative for the dream's sake, but to express his love through "success." Because his will to succeed consistently frustrates his impulse to love, he suffers the division Heilman ascribes to the tragic hero.[12]

In a reversal of Aristotelian priorities Miller dramatizes, in Browning's phrase, "Action in Character, rather than Character in Action." Or, to put it another way, plot enters character to create "the soul of the action" rather than the narrative or external plot. *Death of a Salesman* "removes the ground of the tragic conflict from outer events to inner consciousness," as Esther Merle Jackson has proposed, depicting "a tragedy of consciousness, the imitation of a moral crisis in the life of a common man" (68). This shift violates the linear, architectonic movement of classical tragedy by placing the impetus for the action not in the hands of the gods but in Willy's own consciousness. When he announces "I am tired to death" (2), he sets in motion an inexorable internal struggle between past and present. On the verge of neurosis and paranoia because he vacillates hopelessly between two poles, Willy shares an obsessive nature with other tragic figures who skirt madness. But Miller has always insisted that Willy is not insane. His well-known aversion to Frederic March's portrayal in the film version of the play emphasizes the point. "If he was nuts," Miller wrote of Willy in *Timebends*, "he would hardly stand as a comment on anything" (325). March, who had been a "first choice for the role on stage," made Willy "simply a mental case," a neurotic, pathological case study, "an idiot" headed for the "looney bin," Miller complained to Christopher Bigsby—but Willy is not "crazy," and the audience recognizes that "This man is obviously going down the chute and he's telling them exactly what they believe" (*Arthur Miller*, 54, 58).

The internalization of the conflict is expressed in the staging of the play. We are on "The Inside of His Head," as Miller first proposed calling the work, on a stage expressive of the dialectical tensions between what Miller refers to as "social time" and "psychic time," city and country, home and workplace, as Willy's "daydreams" project the counter forces operating in his consciousness. On one hand, Miller maintained the dictum of tragedy he learned from the Greeks and Ibsen and coined "the birds coming home to roost" (Bigsby, *Arthur Miller*, 49), initiating the play in the rhythm of ancient tragedy with the appearance of "the x-factor" when Willy announces he cannot go on. But from there the play assumes more postmodern traits. As Matthew Roudané has suggested, the text is "Postmodern in texture but gains its theatrical power from ancient echoes, its Hellenic mixture of pity and fear stirring primal emotions" ("*Death of a Salesman*," 63). Although Elia Kazan recognized from the beginning that Willy creates his own history in the play, only recently have critics begun to appreciate Miller's postmodern view of history, an element increasingly apparent in plays like *Some Kind of Love Story*, *Elegy for a Lady*, and more recent works like *The Last Yankee*, *Ride Down Mount Morgan*, and even *Mr. Peter's Connections*. Miller collapses time in *Death of a Salesman*, rather than simply showing the past reasserting itself in the present, making past and present coexist so completely that neither we nor Willy can always distinguish between them. June Schlueter has observed how the extraordinary design "invites a recontextualizing reading of the play and a distinctly postmodern query: To what extent has Willy assumed authorial control of his own history, consciously or unconsciously rewriting and restaging it to suit his emotional needs?" ("Re-membering Willy's Past," 143). In Miller's use of "re-memory," the text challenges "the historicity of knowledge, the nature of identity, the epistemological status of fictional discourse" (151). Yet for all its postmodern elements, as Roudané has rightly asserted, it "gets its power from ancient echoes." Miller began the play with the conviction that "if I could make [Willy] remember enough he would kill himself" (*Theater Essays*, 138). The eruption of the past is vital in this sense because it reflects Miller's tragic view of causality, because it is "an acknowledgment," Christopher Bigsby has declared, "that we are responsible for, and a product of, our actions" ("Introduction," xi).[13]

Inspired by seeing *A Streetcar Named Desire*, Miller developed what Brenda Murphy has termed "subjective realism," which she describes as "expressionistic with the illusion of objectivity afforded by realism" (*Miller: Death of a Salesman*, 5). It allowed him to project a concept of time in which "nothing in life comes 'next' but ... everything exists together at the same time.... [Willy] is his past at every moment." As a result the "form seems to be the form of a confession" (*Theater Essays*, 136). The form thereby conveys the moment of moral consequence when Willy must finally pay the price for his choices—"you've got to retrieve what you've spent and you've got to account for it somehow" (Bigsby, *Arthur Miller*, 201). In fact Miller has employed Biblical language to define the moral significance of the drama, which shows us, "so to speak, the wages of sin" (*Conversations*, 31). Willy, in a way, confesses despite himself as his memory becomes an unwilled confession. As a divided hero he sins against both imperatives that motivate him. He violates the law of success, Miller has explained, "the law which says that a failure in society and in business has no right to live." But he also sins against "an opposing system which, so to speak, is in a race for Willy's faith, and that is the system of love which is the opposite of the law of success" (*Theater Essays*, 149). To be true to one set of values necessitates betrayal of the other. That is the tragic dilemma that Miller traced back to Eden, when either way they choose, either by disobeying the injunction not to eat the fruit or denying their impulse toward freedom, Adam and Eve were fated to suffer tragic consequences. Unable to accommodate diametrically opposite demands, Willy must and does make choices in response to the contending codes. He commits adultery in Boston to gain access to buyers, but consequently carries undeniable guilt for breaking "the law of love." In his annotations to the playscript Miller recorded that Willy is in fact "craving to be liberated from his guilt" (qtd. in Rowe, 56).

It is an essential question whether Willy *does* choose and, perhaps more importantly, whether he truly pays a price for his choices. It is difficult not to see his moral viability in light of his pervasive sense of guilt. Even if he fails to make the right moral choices (though no choice can be "right" in relation to the contending poles in the dialectic), he is surely not amoral. The play demands an accounting for his actions. One may contend that Willy lacks intellectual awareness, of course, and is thereby diminished as a tragic hero, but not that he is morally moribund. Few characters in modern drama expose so vividly the presence of a guilty conscience.

When Willy returns "tired to death," Gerald Weales has concluded, he is "past the point of choice" ("Arthur Miller," 172). In a way he is right. The play begins when Willy must finally suffer "the wages of sin" for choices already made, in the same way that Oedipus must confront the consequences of a crime already enacted. But in fact he also makes choices within the time frame of the present. As Miller has insisted, he is unwilling to "remain passive in the face of what he conceives to be a challenge to his dignity" (*Theater Essays*, 4). To this end he chooses not to take Charley's repeated offer of a job, although he already depends on Charley's help and could resolve his immediate financial crisis by accepting the position. Almost without regard to Willy's rejection of the job, Charley ironically explains why when he remarks at the Requiem, "No man only needs a little salary" (110). Willy chooses not to suffer the loss of dignity—to accept would demean him and, perhaps more, would deny the validity of the imperative by which he measures his worth. Most importantly, he chooses the car at the end of the play over the rubber hose, the latter representing both acceptance of defeat and escape from the consequences of failure, the former embodying an act of sacrifice, an ironic affirmation of the failed dream but, nonetheless, a conscious assertion of will. As will be discussed later, suicide by means of the rubber hose constitutes death *from* something, suicide by car death *for* something. Without free will tragedy cannot exist in Miller's view, for tragedy contests the idea that characters are only victims of external powers rather than participants in their own destiny. Just as we can conclude that Willy is morally alive, we must acknowledge that he possesses freedom of choice. He chose to follow the imperative that finally defeats him, and he chooses to die in part to perpetuate the dream. "He brings tragedy down on himself," Raymond Williams has explained in his defense of the play as tragedy, "not by opposing the lie, but by living it" (104).

Willy might be considered a composite tragic hero in that his divided nature and tragic fate are inexplicably bound to his two sons, who represent the poles in the dialectic. Willy's choice to follow the dictates of the cultural ethos most directly affects his family, which provides the locus of the tragic action. The larger community and its unifying myth of universal order are projected in the altar, the palace, and the throne-room in traditional tragedy; but the fragile Loman house, part externally real and part psychically real, houses a fragmented, dysfunctional family, where Willy's adherence to the law of success makes him, as Dan Vogel has noted, a petty "tyrannos" in his own house. But whereas "the family was subsumed by community, by public and even metaphysical-religious repercussions" in Greek drama, William Demastes has reminded us, in the Loman household family matters are disconnected from the larger human society or a spiritually charged cosmos (77). Though Shakespeare's heroes all engage in psychological warfare at some personal level, they all see themselves as primarily agents of the larger community. Oedipus's or Hamlet's "Oedipus Complex" is hardly the "soul of the action" in either text, however much both may be perceived in Freudian terms. But Miller has spoken of family in overtly Freudian terms as, "after all, the nursery of all our neuroses" (*Conversations*, 271), moving tragedy much more into the realm of the psyche and subjective reality as O'Neill tried to do. Some critics, and most notably the psychiatrist Daniel E.

Schneider, have read the play as centrally about the Oedipus complex, "an unreal Oedipal bloodbath," in which we witness the search for the father, violent sibling rivalry, castration fear, and crippling guilt over the death of a parent.[14] But while such themes doubtless appear, the rivalry between brothers and their struggles against the father are more important as manifestations of larger mythic forces operating in Willy himself. Biff's association with nature and desire to return to a pastoral world characterized by fecundity and openness parallel Willy's lyrical references to New England, the open windshield and the warm air early in the play and, later in the play, his promise to Linda to someday buy a farm and his desperate attempt to "plant something." Hap's counter-commitment to the idea of success, seen throughout in his unconscionable business dealings and sexual prowess, reaches full expression at the Requiem in his vow to reclaim Willy's dream. But because Willy still naively convinces himself that he will eventually succeed and never doubts the dream Hap embodies, Willy does not need the assurances of his younger son or his forgiveness for not having been a success. It is Biff with whom he must be reconciled for the breech caused by his denial of "the system of love," a denial of his own other self.

Brenda Murphy has noted Miller's evolving conception of Biff. At first seeing the elder son as caught "between hatred for Willy and his own desire for success," the playwright had difficulty "developing a motivation for Biff's hatred" (*Miller: Death of a Salesman*, 9). But especially under Kazan's direction, Miller came to see the work, in Kazan's words, as "a love story—the end of a tragic love between Willy and his son Biff.... The whole play is about *love*—Love and Competition" (qtd. in Rowe, 44).[15] When the Chinese actor playing Biff in Beijing wondered why Biff says "I don't know what I want," Miller, in a telling comment, replied,

> You don't say "I don't know what I want," but "I don't know what I'm supposed to want," and this is a key idea. Biff knows very well what he wants, but Willy and his idea of success disapprove of what he wants, and this is the basic reason you have returned here—to somehow resolve this conflict with your father, to get his blessing. (*Salesman*, 71)

Willy and Biff form a symbiotic relationship. Biff cannot gain freedom from his father's imperative until his father somehow frees him from it—as, tragically speaking, he can do only through death. Similarly, Willy cannot succeed until he can align his love for Biff with the dream he follows. This explains that Biff returns because, as Miller explained to the Beijing actors, he "sometimes feels a painful unrequited love for his father, a sense of something unfinished between them brings feelings of guilt" (*Salesman*, 79). Willy equally feels "unrequited love," which we see in his eagerness for Biff's return, and yet he also suffers "feelings of guilt." Biff has failed to meet Willy's imperative and feels estranged because of it; Willy has violated love for the sake of the dream by which he hoped to express it and feels alienated as well. Inextricably linked, both in Willy's subjective world where he romanticizes Biff in the past to conform to his dream and in the external realm of reality where Biff has markedly failed to succeed, the two return to the crossroads, the place where *x* marks the spot, the hotel room in Boston where the law of success and the law of love collided, inflicting upon father and son a shared guilt that can only be redeemed by the death of the tragic hero.

Like the Greek chorus whose plea for relief unwittingly leads to Oedipus's tragic end, Linda's supplications propel Willy and Biff toward their tragic destiny. As she tells her son, "Biff, his life is in your hands!" (43). Yet from the beginning Linda has provoked intense critical reactions. Many see her as an enabler who "contributes to the truth–illusion matrix" by supporting Willy's "vital lie" (Roudané, "*Death of a Salesman*," 70).[16] Some consider her an even more sinister figure. Guerin Bliquez has called her "the source of the cash-payment fixation" whose acquiescence "in all Willy's weaknesses" makes her a "failure as a wife and mother." Seeing Ben as a rival, Bliquez adds, she emasculates and makes Willy a victim of her "ambition as well as his own" (384, 386). Calling her "stupid and immoral" for encouraging Willy's self-deceit, Brian Parker accuses Linda of possessing no higher ideal than Willy's dream and finds her "moral sloppiness" manifested in Hap "one degree farther"—"Hap is his mother's son" (54). And Karl Harshbarger makes her an even more malevolent character who coerces Willy "to relate to her as a small boy ... by not allowing him to communicate his deeper needs to her," sides with Biff against him, and blames him "for his own feelings. She offers him his reward, love and support, only when he becomes dependent on her" (14). He goes so far as to claim that in her "extreme defensiveness" against her own guilt she "must disguise the joy that she, not a man, has been victorious" (28).[17] Linda is also commonly referred to as merely a sentimental sop, a cardboard figure, or "a mouthpiece for Miller's earnestness" (Welland, 50). One critic has named her Jocasta, a "mousy twentieth-century Brooklyn housewife" who, like Oedipus's wife-mother, prevents her husband "from asking the fatal question, 'Who am I?'" (C. Otten, 87).

More recent feminist critics have found Linda a likely target for assaults on Miller, though as early as his 1970 book on Miller, Benjamin Nelson sounded a feminist chord that shows Linda helping "build a doll's house around [Willy] and, consequently, [doing] to Willy what he has been doing to Biff and Happy," making him as well as them "victims of her gingerbread house" (112–13).[18] A number of studies published in the late 1980s deny Linda a significant role in a tragic pattern, depicting her as reflecting a male perspective, which "borrows the methods and espouses the sexual politics of melodrama.... If Miller writes tragedy ... he makes it a male preserve" (Mason, 113). Linda, according to Linda Ben-Zvi, "is the embodiment of society's perception of women" and of Miller's own conception (224), a view shared by Gayle Austin. Employing the feminist theory of Gayle Rubin, Austin laments Miller's reduction of women as "objects to be exchanged" and denial of them "as active subjects in the play" (61, 63). And Kay Stanton concludes that Miller conflates all female characters in the play "in the idea of Woman: all share ... in their knowing"; and possessing "the potential to reveal masculine inadequacy," they "must be opposed by man" (82).[19] More recently, Linda Kintz has explored Miller's "grammar of space," which projects "a nostalgic view of the universalized masculine protagonist of the Poetics," in which conception women like Linda "wait at home, to console and civilize both husband and children, roles that provide a structural, narrative guarantee of masculine agency even in very different historical periods" (106). Tracing anti-female bias to the core of traditional tragedy itself, she raises a serious criticism not only of Linda's role but of the gender-biased nature of tragedy as genre.

These and other feminist attacks on the characterization of Linda and the other women in the play[20] have not gone unchallenged; and relative to seeing the play as tragedy, the issue is important, because Miller conceives of Linda as an essential contributor to the tragic meaning of work. Jan Balakian, for example, has argued that, rather than supporting a sexist view of women, *Death of a Salesman* in "accurately depicting a postwar American culture that subordinates women, ... cries out for a renewed image of American women" (115). Although the drama realistically portrays America "through the male gaze," it "does not condone the locker-room treatment of women any more than it approves of a dehumanizing capitalism, any more than *A Streetcar Named Desire* approves Stanley Kowalski's brash chauvinism or David Mamet's *Glengarry Glen Ross* approves of sleazy real-estate salesmen" (124). Even if Linda's fierce will and love for Willy cannot save him, Christopher Bigsby has added, "this does not make her a 'useful doormat'" as some feminists have complained ("Introduction," xx).

As Elia Kazan wrote in his directing notes on the play, Linda often appears as if she is ideally "fashioned out of Willy's guilt" and male ego as "Hard-working, sweet, always true, admiring.... Dumb, slaving, tender, innocent." In fact, "in life she is much tougher ... she has *chosen* Willy! To hell with everyone else. She is terrifyingly tough" (qtd. in Rowe, 47). Certainly Miller did not think of her as a sentimental sop. Kay Stanton has suggested that Miller "seems not to have fully understood" her strength as a "common woman who possesses more tragic nobility than Willy" (96), but at various times Miller has expressed his concern that Linda not be sentimentalized, beginning with Mildred Dunnock's original portrayal of the role.[21] He recalled how Kazan forced Dunnock to deliver her long accusatory speech to Bill and Happy in Act II in double time and then doubled the pace of the delivery again in order to straighten "out her spine, and has Linda filled up with outrage and protest rather than self-pity and mere perplexity" (*Timebends*, 189). He also observed how the Linda in the Beijing production, Zhu Lin, at first weakened Linda's character by "exploiting ... the sentiments" that "will sink them all in a morass of brainless 'feeling' that finally is not feeling at all but an unspecific bath of self-love." Zhu Lin's interpretation reminded him of a Yiddish production in New York in which "the Mother was a lachrymose fount" like mothers "performed by actors of Irish backgrounds" in early film, "always on the verge of tears, too" (*Salesman*, 43).

For Miller, Linda's role was never merely ancillary. And although he acknowledged that she contributes to Willy's death—noting that "When somebody is destroyed, everybody finally contributes to it" (*Conversations*, 265), he conceived of Linda as "sucked into the same mechanism" as Willy.[22] Though not a "tragic hero," Linda contributes hugely to the tragic vision of the work. She functions in part as a chorus. In the crucial moments when she demands that "Attention must be paid" and when she castigates her sons for abandoning Willy, she both provokes the action and provides a moral commentary on it. Perhaps more, as George Couchman has contributed, she "is conscience itself" to her two sons—"she fixes responsibility for actions, something which, according to the playwright himself, must be done if our theater is to recover the spirit of tragedy" (74). And, Bernard Dukore has added, "Far from demonstrating her stupidity, her comprehension of why [Willy] committed suicide derives from what she, not the audience, was aware of. When she last saw Willy, he was happy because Biff loved him" (28). Her essential recognition, though emotionally rather than intellectually expressed, illuminates the tragic implications of the text.

No mere passive victim, even though she is powerless to prevent Willy's end, Linda is primarily responsible for generating the tragic reunion of Willy and Biff. She can only respond to, not prevent, the fatal encounter she unwittingly prophesies when she tells Biff, with ironic accuracy, that Willy's fate is in his hands; and it is she who tells Biff about the rubber hose, thereby empowering him with the knowledge he needs to confront Willy at the end of the play. The climactic scene occurs at the restaurant when Willy can no longer evade the memory that must return him, like Oedipus, to the crossroads that mark his betrayal. The scene in Howard's office which precedes it would surely be the pivotal moment in the action were this essentially a social or political drama; but rather than being the turning point, it leads directly to it, stripping Willy of his final hope and leaving him without reserves to combat the evidence of his failure as father and husband as well as salesman.[23] Christopher Bigsby has proposed that "There is no crime and hence no culpability (beyond guilt for sexual betrayal), only a baffled man and his sons trying to find their way through a world of images" ("Introduction," xxvi); but the guilt Willy endures goes beyond mere infidelity, and Biff's culpability in abandoning his father both in Boston and at the restaurant adds a moral dimension that exceeds Willy's sexual indiscretions. The restaurant scene, which Miller once stayed up all night to rework during rehearsals (*Timebends*, 189), brilliantly weaves together past and present by simultaneously showing Biff and Hap reenacting Willy's violation of love while Willy concurrently relives it. Again, were this only a social or polemical social play, the scene in Howard's office would constitute the nadir of Willy's hopeless existence, and the restaurant scene would begin the dénouement. But the restaurant scene carries what Miller calls a "metaphysical" dimension, moving the play into the realm of tragedy by dramatizing the usurpation of the present by the past, the place where Willy must reenact rather than excuse or sanitize the past. In true tragic rhythm, every step forward leads back to that defining moment.

Biff's humiliating experience at Oliver's office mirrors Willy's at Howard's, Thomas Porter has noted (142), and links their destinies together as they meet at the restaurant. The scene opens with Hap seducing "Miss Forsyth" with the deception and exaggeration typical of the Lomans, directly establishing a parallel to Willy's sexual infidelity. When Biff arrives, he already has realized his inauthenticity after stealing Oliver's pen and is determined to force Willy and Hap to face the truth about all their self-deceit. Interestingly, Miller changed the early versions of the play, including the initial preproduction script distributed to the production team in 1948. Originally Biff intentionally lies both to Willy and Hap about having a lunch meeting with Oliver (Murphy, *Miller: Death of a Salesman*, 6). In the far more meaningful final version, Biff openly rebels against what he has become. Daniel Schneider, in his Freudian interpretation of the scene, calls it "the ultimate act of father-murder ... [a] very adroitly designed Oedipal murder" in which Biff is "hero of the Oedipal theme" in rebelling against his father (250–51).[24] But while Biff comes in anger against what his father has made of him and does indeed rebel against him, he brings with him a deeper self-hatred and, with it, an understanding of Willy's desperation. Even as Hap competes for the girls unmindful of his father's distress, Biff finds a compassion born of his self-awareness and Willy's agonizing cry that "the woods are burning ... there's a big blaze going on all around" (83). Biff's consciousness of his own culpability—expressed in his plea to Hap to "help him.... Help me, help me, I can't bear to look at his face!"—bespeaks of something more than Oedipal revenge on the father. Calling Willy "A fine, troubled prince" (90), he lies about the appointment with Oliver not to conceal his failure, as in the original script, but to alleviate Willy's suffering, even though he finally runs away from Willy in frustration, "*Ready to weep*" (90). Biff wants to be free of the past and free of the imperative of success his father imposes on him, but he cannot achieve these ends without feeling guilt for failing his father, nor can he erase from the past the estrangement that occurred in Boston for which he feels partly responsible. In this modern tragedy, moral as well as psychological forces propel the scene.

As tragic protagonist Willy, above all, must gain some measure of awareness, something now possible when he no longer possesses the capacity to reinvent, glamorize, or excuse the past. The "re-memory" of the experience in the hotel room is driven by guilt left unchecked without recourse to the defensive mechanisms of deceit and denial he has always employed. Consciously trying to fend off responsibility, he told Bernard at Charley's office that the math teacher, "that son-of-a-bitch," destroyed Biff, but he knows subconsciously Biff "laid down and died like a hammer hit him" because he lost all will when he caught Willy with the secretary (71). Willy's anger at Linda's mending stockings makes apparent his inability to wash his hands of guilt as well. His infidelity, echoed by Biff's prowess as a teenager and Hap's exploitation of his competitors' women, is ironically fused with its opposite. The same sexual exploits which violate "the system of love" Miller alludes to are a means to fulfill the imperative of success, whose ultimate end for Willy is, paradoxically, to secure the family and assert his fatherhood. The merging of Linda's laughter with that of the woman in the hotel represents the fatal union of imperative and impulse in Willy's mind; he is now unable to separate the contending forces that propel him. The sexual encounter with the woman is not the cause of Willy's violation of his love for Linda or his sons but the symptom of a tragic conflict which he has, nonetheless, created. However much Willy struggles to live in denial consciously, he knows subconsciously that he bears responsibility, as his suffering bears witness. The play shifts after the restaurant scene into the future and out of Willy's unconscious, as Willy, having returned to the point of offense, seeks for some means to reconcile the conflicting "laws" that define him. The dénouement inevitably follows the subjective reenactment of the encounter his memory will not let him evade—once again, "the birds come home to roost."

To what degree Willy really understands and accepts responsibility is a matter of unending debate among critics. In his prefatory essay to his *Collected Works*, Miller argued that

> Had Willy been unaware of his separation from values that endure he would have died contentedly polishing his car.... But he was agonized by being in a false position, so constantly haunted by the hollowness of all he had put his faith in.... That he had not intellectual fluency to verbalize his situation is not the same as saying that he lacked awareness. (*Theater Essays*, 148)

Nevertheless, in an earlier interview he acknowledged the "danger in pathos, which can destroy any tragedy if it goes too far," and confessed, "I feel that Willy Loman lacks sufficient insight into his situation, which would have made him a greater, more significant figure" (*Conversations*, 26). Miller's detractors, and in some cases defenders, have focused on this issue. Heilman, for example, has written that *Death of a Salesman* is a near-but-not-quite-tragedy because "Willy is always in the first stage of the tragic rhythm—the flight from the truth; but he never comes to the last stage of the tragic rhythm, in which truth breaks through to him" (234). And June Schlueter has argued that although Willy "casts an immense shadow over all of modern drama, he remains a pathetic 'low man'" (Schlueter and Flanagan, 63).[25]

But even granting Willy's limited insight, it would be a mistake to claim that he is ignorant of himself or of his moral offenses. Certainly emotionally, as Lois Gordon contends, "he confronts himself and his world" (103). Roudané persuasively argues that Willy "tragically knows at least part of himself" as is evidenced when he admits to Linda that he looks foolish, that he babbles too much, and that he feels estranged. He "mixes self-disclosure with external fact," as when he sarcastically responds to Hap, "You'll retire me for life on seventy goddam dollars a week?" And his lyric cry, "The woods are burning!" further reflects Willy's "self-knowledge within the marketplace" as "he honestly assesses his overall predicament" when he meets his sons at the restaurant. "Such insights make Willy more than a misfit or an oversimplified Everyman" and "enhance his tragic structure precisely because they reveal to the audience Willy's capacity to distinguish reality from chimera" ("*Death of a Salesman*," 79). Granting that Willy himself does not comprehend the full meaning of his spiritual crisis or his guilt, Bernard Dukore asks, What if he did fully understand? "The play would then become too explicit and Willy the know-it-all protagonist of a drama with Uplift" (37), devoid of tragic significance and at odds with the play's realistic portrayal.

Miller's commitment to the truthfulness of Willy's character in effect mitigates against his playing the role of the classical tragic hero—he "knows" in the Old Testament sense of experiencing reality, but there is no doubt that his intellectual vision is restricted. When he leaves the restaurant shattered by his painful return to the Boston hotel room, Willy is to a degree freed to act, to choose. Before his mental reenactment he was incapacitated by Howard's final humiliation of him, by his agonizing awareness that Bernard's success reflected on his own failure as father, by Charley's offer of a job that would come at the cost of any self-respect. Now he is galvanized into desperate action. Mobilized by the stinging awareness that he has utterly failed materially and morally, he impulsively tries to plant something, to nurture life amid walls of urban apartment houses that symbolize the domination of the nature he loves by the material world created by the selling mythos of American culture to which he is hopelessly tied.

His actions expose his sense of, rather than understanding of, his existential dilemma. In Miller's view of a world without transcendent mythic heroes, Willy alone cannot embody the tragic vision of the play. As part of a composite tragic figure, Biff assumes a dimension of the tragic protagonist Willy is too diminished to satisfy. As a projection of competing forces operating in Willy's psyche, Biff seeks freedom from the "phony dream" that he nonetheless carries as symbolically part of Willy. Joseph Hynes has expressed dismay that "The only one who gains self-awareness is Biff; but the play is Willy's.... [T]he showdown lights up the play's failure as tragedy" (286). But in fact the play does not turn on Willy as a single protagonist. Because Willy is so wedded to the dream, nothing less than his death can free him from it. Biff, however, can acquire freedom from the imperative Willy cannot abandon without self-destruction; but, paradoxically, he can only be freed *by* Willy. Possessing awareness of the corrosive nature of Willy's dream and its devastating effect on his father and himself, Biff pleads with Willy to "take that phony dream and burn it" (106). The "*anagnorisis* is there," declares David Sievers, but "is given ... to Biff, who is purged of his father's hostility when he comes to see his father for what he is" (396). When he expresses his love for his father in a climactic embrace, he frees Willy to claim his tragic fate, as, paradoxically, Willy's death frees him.

Biff, then, provides the awareness Willy lacks, but he cannot himself resolve the tragic crisis. It may be true that Miller does not adequately develop Biff's character in relation to Willy or fully trace his moral development, although it is clear from the beginning that Biff returns home because he feels a sense of guilt and moral responsibility to heal the breech with his father. Miller himself has stated, "I am sorry the self-realization of the older son, Biff, is not a weightier counterbalance of Willy's character" (*Theater Essays*, 9–10), but his intent is not obscure. Biff is not a counterweight *to* but a counterweight *of* Willy's character. However unwittingly, Willy pays the price to free Biff from the imperative he ironically thinks he dies to defend: "[T]ragedy brings *us* knowledge and enlightenment" as audience, Dukore has wisely remarked, "which it need not do for the tragic hero" (37).

It is hardly surprising that the motivation for Willy's suicide is variously interpreted, for Miller himself substantially altered his earlier depiction of the death. The earlier version of the penultimate scene, Brenda Murphy has noted, occurs not when Biff confronts Willy with the rubber hose but when he confesses for the first time that he lied about the appointment with Oliver (*Miller: Death of a Salesman*, 6). The difference is important because the rubber hose, like the car accidents earlier, reveals Willy's flirtation with surrender to defeat. The car wrecks "were cowardly and escapist," Dan Vogel has rightly claimed, whereas his death at the end of the play is "purposeful, self-sacrificial, and epiphanic" (101). Although it does nothing to achieve Willy's dream, it is not, as June Schlueter has concluded, simply "a deluded death gesture that only compounds the waste of his life" (Schlueter and Flanagan, 65). Miller has identified the cause as Willy's "epiphany" in the penultimate scene when he realizes "He loves me!" and discovers "the resurrected knowledge of his vision with Biff, his seed and hope" (*Salesman*, 170). Having gained "a very powerful piece of knowledge, which is that he is loved by his son and has been embraced by him and forgiven," he can now choose death as fulfillment, not mere escape:

> That he is unable to take the victory thoroughly to his heart, that it closes the circle for him and propels him to his death, is the wage of sin, which was to have committed himself so completely to the counterfeits of dignity and the false coinage embodied in his idea of success that he can prove his existence only by bestowing "power" on his posterity, a power deriving from the sale of his last asset, himself, for the price of his insurance policy. (*Theater Essays*, 147)

The point is that Willy, however wrongly, chooses to die in such a way that he believes can restore the equilibrium between the imperative of success and the contesting will to love. "Unwittingly," Miller has written, "he has primed his own son Biff for his revolt against what he himself has done with his life and against what he has come to worship: material success" (*Salesman*,

135).[26] Anything less than death would make Willy's end purely melodramatic. As Kazan recorded, "it is a *deed*, not a feeling" (qtd. in Rowe, 49)—that Willy *chooses* rather than succumbs makes all the difference. In "The Nature of Tragedy" (1949), Miller wrote that "When Mr. B., while walking down the street, is struck on the head by a falling piano," we witness "only the pathetic end of Mr. B. .... [T]he death of Mr. B. does not arouse ... tragic feeling" and produces no catharsis (*Theater Essays*, 9). Willy's death is neither accidental nor senseless. That he dies *for* something, however misconstrued, rather than *from* debilitating defeat makes his end meaningful—and necessary. His death eliminates Biff's obligation to conform to his father's ideal. Although Christopher Bigsby is right in claiming that it is not "truth" but Willy's "commitment to illusion" that kills him (*Critical Introduction*, 179), the consummate irony is that he frees Biff from the very idea he holds in absolute allegiance. In the final analysis, the dream of success is not Willy's "ultimate concern" but a corruptive means to a higher end. That Willy remains ignorant of the truth that the dream subverts his end to reestablish the love between him and his son does not erase the fact that he dies as the agent of that love.

The effectiveness of the Requiem has been another point of contention among critics: to some it is contrived and extraneous to the rest of the play, to others a necessary commentary on the consequences of the action. Miller has described a distinct breakpoint at the end of the drama. When Willy "dies his consciousness vanishes and there is a space between the requiem and the play.... We've left Willy's head now; we're on the earth" (Bigsby, *Arthur Miller*, 59). In his view, crossing the distance between Willy's distorted internal point of view to external reality is essential to the resolution of the play. Without the Requiem there would be only the death of a self-deluded salesman whose end achieves nothing but blind self-annihilation. Willy's "tragedy" would provoke, as George Jean Nathan described it in his famous review of the play, an "experience [like] we suffer in contemplating on the highways a run-over and killed dog, undeniably affecting but without any profound significance" (284). Miller, though, does not portray Willy's death as meaningless, though it is certainly ironic. He has written, "We have abstracted from the Greek drama its air of doom, its physical destruction of the hero, but its victory escapes us. Thus it has become difficult to separate in our minds the ideas of the pathetic and of the tragic" (*Theater Essays*, 59).

In *Death of a Salesman* he attempts to conjoin the pathetic and the tragic in a unique way by uniting the destinies of Biff and Willy. Chester Eisinger has argued that Biff's recognition "provides the contrapuntal release to life that we must see over against Willy's defeat in suicide" (171). But, in a larger sense, Biff's epiphany—that "I know who I am kid" (111)—is not one thing and Willy's death another, not a point/counterpoint but an integrated whole. Miller has acknowledged the seeming "rift" in the play between the focus of the dramatic action which falls on Willy and the recognition and moral resolution which fall on Biff. He knew he could not give Willy Biff's insight and be true to Willy's character, which is why he considered the funeral essential to rescue the play from pessimism. Willy's last conversation with Ben keeps his illusion intact,[27] but the Requiem enlarges the vision. You go to a funeral because "You want to think over the life of the departed and it's then, really, that it's nailed down: [Biff] won't accept his life" (Bigsby, *Arthur Miller*, 56). Willy gains emotional awareness of Biff's love and consequently finds self-worth in dying for that love; Biff discovers freeing self-knowledge. His decision to go West may represent, as Nada Zeineddine has suggested, a "metaphorically killing of the father" (178), a last expression of Oedipal rebellion against the father.[28] Biff confidently asserts that Willy "had the wrong dreams. All, all wrong" (111). His rejection of his father's ideal, however, emerges paradoxically from his embrace of his father and his father's ultimate act of love for him.

There is more uncertainty, more lack of resolve, at the end of the play than we ordinarily find in most conventional tragedies. Biff's heading West, Christopher Bigsby has written, "smacks a little of Huck Finn lighting out for the Territory, ahead of the rest. He is moving against history" ("Introduction," xix). And both Bigsby and Gerald Weales have noted the irony that Biff's return to the West foreshadows the cowboy Gay's fate in *The Misfits*, who is displaced in the dying agrarian society (*Modern American Drama*, 90; "Arthur Miller," 178).[29] Weales also has concluded that "there is no reason to assume that some of the irony" directed to Willy and the other Lomans "does not rub off on Biff" ("Arthur Miller," 169). Nevertheless, Biff most certainly moves "from something and to something." As he developed Biff's character, Miller clearly intended to show that Biff gains independence from, rather than perpetuates, his father's life of illusion. Bernard Dukore has implied that it is good that Miller does not more fully counterbalance Biff's perception against Willy's blindness, because the play "might then become an italicized message." Those who say Biff's vision is "vague, trite and romantic, miss the point" (25). The tragic vision does not depend on being able to predict what will happen to Biff so much as on our awareness that Willy's death dissolves Biff's obligation to meet a spurious ideal, whatever the sequel might say.

Other parts of the Requiem have also been debated vigorously. Charley's "A salesman is got to dream" speech has been variously called out of character and realistic,[30] and Linda's often discussed last words "we're free

.... We're free ..." (12) have been dismissed as a trite appeal for sympathy and too obvious irony.[31] One might ask what the essential irony is, that Linda thinks they are free when they are not or that they are free more than Linda knows—freed from the fear of Willy's death and freed from his illusory ideal. While some, like Ruby Cohn, have accused the Requiem of being "jarringly outside" Willy's mind and devoid of any new insights, it introduces a metaphysical dimension at the end. Rita Di Giuseppe has proposed that Linda's remark about the insurance, "It's the grace period now," gives "the jargon of commerce ... a metaphysical connotation" (126). And one might add that Miller considered calling the play *A Period of Grace*, as if to emphasize something transcendent that emerges in it.

What we are left with is perhaps a tragedy despite itself—Willy is a victim, but chooses nonetheless; he lacks self-knowledge, but is responsible for his son's self-awareness; his ideal is all wrong, but his commitment to it is aligned with a love he willingly dies for; his death lifts no plague and does not affect the larger community, but it rescues his family from the continuing anxiety of his death and releases Biff from a destructive imperative. Willy is petty, delusional, pathetic; but "Attention, attention must be finally paid to such a person" (43). However circuitously, the play completes the tragic pattern of the past becoming the present, and it affirms the tragic dictum that there are inevitable consequences to choices, that the "the wages of sin" must be paid. Lacking a singular tragic protagonist, it offers a composite figure of father and sons who embody the tragic conflict between the imperative of success and the "system of love." Leaving society unredeemed, it ends in sacrifice to reclaim the family and restore love. Not "high tragedy" in Aristotelian terms, *Death of a Salesman* is something more than melodrama or "low tragedy" in its revelation of tragic vision, choice, awareness, and consequence. At fifty years of age, Miller's play is still "coming home to roost."

NOTES

1. Miller earlier told Robert Corrigan that he was not "concerned about tragic form" in writing the play: "That is after the fact. Just to lay that to rest. The theatre gets too involved in analytical theory" (*Conversations*, 257).

2. He also has described the play as "absurdly simple! It is about a salesman and it's his last day on the earth" (*Theater Essays*, 423).

3. Miller also told James J. Martine his often repeated admission that the Greeks and Ibsen were the "two sources for my form—certainly for my ideas of a theatre's purposes" (*Conversations*, 292). He told Olga Carlisle and Rose Styron in a *Paris Review* interview published in 1966 that tragedy "seemed to me the only form there was" when he began writing drama and that he especially admired the Greeks "for their magnificent form, the symmetry.... That form has never left me; I suppose it got burned into me" (*Conversations*,

88). He also called himself a "descendent of Ibsen" in an interview with Ronald Hyman: "What he gave me in the beginning was a sense of the past and a sense of the rootedness of everything that happens" (*Conversations*, 189).

4. All citations to *Death of a Salesman* refer to this edition.

5. For a general summary of major opening-night reviews of the play as "tragedy," see especially Murphy, *Miller: Death of a Salesman*, 61–65. Articles and books that directly address the question tend to include summaries of critical opinions on the topic. For an especially useful commentary placing the play against historical definitions of tragedy, see Barker "The Crisis of Authenticity," particularly his pithy but useful appendix tracing the evolution of theoretical views of tragedy.

6. For more sustained discussions of *Death of a Salesman* and *Oedipus*, see especially Siegel; C. Otten; Bhatia; Bierman, Hart, and Johnson; Jackson.

7. Among those measuring Miller against Aristotle, Rita Di Giuseppe argues most extensively and convincingly that *Death of a Salesman* is a modern Aristotelian tragedy. Her essay might be compared with Stephen Barker's provocative reading of the play in "The Crisis of Authenticity," which treats it as an essentially Nietzschean tragedy.

8. Heilman himself concludes that Willy is "so limited that this is a limitation of the play itself" (*Tragedy and Melodrama*, 237), a common view of many critics who identify the play with Aristotelian "low tragedy."

9. The theologian-literary critic Tom Driver, for example, complains that "There being no objective good and evil, and no imperative other than conscience, man himself must be made to bear the full burden of creating his values and living up to them. The immensity of this task is beyond human capacity" (111–12). In fact, Miller's depiction of the moral viability of characters surfaces in their pervasive sense of guilt and the compulsion shared by Willy and Biff to somehow redeem the past. Driver, like Foster and Mottram, among others, seemingly expects Miller to manufacture a god, a metaphysical reality that would somehow resolve the spiritual crisis. But Miller's refusal to identify "an ultimate truth" is more a matter of artistic integrity than a failure of moral vision.

10. John Manders identifies a related unresolved conflict between Marxist and Freudian elements: "If we take the 'psychological' motivation as primary, the 'social' documentation seem gratuitous; if we take the 'social' documentation as primary, the 'psychological' motivation seems gratuitous" (115).

11. In Helene Koon's words, "His principles may be unconscious and built upon fallacies, but he believes in them, practices them, and finally dies for them" (7).

12. Bernard F. Dukore asks the telling question, "does not the desire for love inhere in Willy's occupation, and does not the hope of success link to the family?" (21)

13. In *Modern American Drama 1945–1990* Bigsby has written, "the present cannot be severed from the past nor the individual from his social context: that, after all, is the basis of [Miller's] dramatic method and of his moral faith" (124).

14. Freudian readings appear incidentally in various interpretations of the play as well as being the primary approach of many studies like Schneider's. See especially Field, Hagopian, Harshbarger, and Schlueter and Flanagan.

15. Miller described the play in similar language: "*Death of a Salesman*, really, is a love story between a man and his son" (*Salesman*, 49).

16. Donald Morse also has noted Linda's reinforcement of Willy's "life-lie" (273–77). And William Dillingham, among others, has identified her as a "contributing cause" of the tragedy (344).

17. In his extreme psychological reading Harshbarger argues that Linda dominates Willy and attempts to reduce Biff "to the level of a dependent child" motivated by "a

longing for Biff she has always had—a relationship which is symbolized by Biff taking '*her in his arms*'" at the end of the play (28–29).

18. Related to feminist criticism, David Savran attacks the play from a different gender perspective, claiming that "the play eulogizes the contents of the Loman *imaginaire* by its romantization of a self-reliant and staunchly homosocial masculinity and by its corroborative and profound disparagement of women" (36).

19. In a recent article Rhonda Koenig concurs that Miller diminishes female figures, making Linda "a dumb and useful doormat" and reducing all women in the play to either the "wicked slut" or "a combination of good waitress and slipper-bearing retriever" (10, 4).

20. For other feminist interpretations see especially Billman, Canning, Goodman, Hume, and Zeineddine.

21. Even in writing the play Miller was intent on showing Linda's toughness. He even cut the famous "Attention must be paid speech" at one point for fear it made her too sentimental, and he took out of the original dialogue references she made to Biff and Hap as "darling" and "dear" (Murphy, *Miller: Death of a Salesman*, 45).

22. Elsewhere he has commented that "There is a more sinister side to the women characters in my plays.... [T]hey both receive the benefits of the male's mistakes and protect his mistakes in crazy ways. They are forced to do that. So the females are victims as well" (*Conversations*, 370).

23. Bernard Dukore rightly comments that even if Howard had given Willy a job in the city, it would not eliminate "the elemental source of Willy's discontent, which lies in his relationship with his older son and the world in which they live" (34). One might add that Willy cannot accept Charley's offer of a job for much the same reason. It would not resolve his existential crisis, and Willy's acceptance of it would in fact reduce him to a totally pathetic figure.

24. Field, Eisinger, and Harshbarger offer other Freudian analyses. Some critics especially note the Freudian importance of Biff's stealing Oliver's pen, a phallic symbol, thus expressing his assertion of manhood or fear of castration. More simply, the stealing of the pen is another re-enactment of the past, when Biff stole the basketballs, like he stole lumber and the football. His existential self-questioning of his motives for stealing the pen makes him determined to coerce Willy to confront the truth about who he really is.

25. Miller has denied that he intended the name as a pun, claiming he took it from a character in Fritz Lang's early film *The Testament of Mr. Mabuse* (*Timebends*, 177).

26. In the same essay Miller has claimed, "Willy is indeed going toward something through his dying, a meaningful sacrifice, the ultimate irony, and he is filled, not emptied of feeling" (196).

27. Ben represents the most corrupt form of the American dream of success, what Thomas Porter has called "the older version of the Salesman, the ruthless capitalist" whose adventuresome brutality contrasts with Willy's "Dale Carnegie approach to success" (135), most fully idealized in Willy's vision of Dave Singleman. But Ben is also Willy's alter ego, as Sister M. Bettina, SSND, has discussed, "a projection of his brother's personality" whose presence provides "a considerable amount of tragic insight" (83). Willy's dependency on Ben's approval stems from his brother being a substitute father and the sole link to their peddler-father, who sold what he created with his own hands in opposition to Ben, who entered the virulent "jungle" and ripped out the riches. Rita Di Giuseppe has drawn the interesting conclusion that Ben functions "much in the same manner as the 'gods' in classical tragedy who hover in the twilight zone uttering prophesies" (117), both the embodiment of the success myth and its arbitrator.

28. Roudané has agreed that Biff "still carries on an Oedipal resistance to his father" at the Requiem (*Death of a Salesman*, 81).

29. In his *Critical Introduction to American Drama* Bigsby has alluded to Gay as an aging cowboy, as bewildered by the collapse of his world as Willy Loman has been" (185). Other critics, like Eisinger, have similarly contended that Miller sentimentally "romanticizes the rural-agrarian dream" (174).

30. For example, Joseph Hynes has dismissed the speech as "sheer sentimentality" and "untrue" (283), whereas Dennis Welland has claimed that Charley alone understands Willy as salesman "in a wholly unsentimental way" (42). Miller himself considered the speech "objective information ... it is absolutely real" and presents the obverse of Charley's earlier remark, "'Why must everybody like you. Who liked J. P. Morgan?' ... These are two halves of the same thing" (*Conversations*, 351–52). As several critics have noted, Miller's sympathetic portrayal of Charley as successful businessman, father, and neighbor, mitigates against simplistically reading the play as an attack on American capitalism.

31. Joseph Hynes, for example, has described Linda and Charley's words as a "Hallmark Card flourish at the curtain" (284).

WORKS CITED

Austin, Gayle. "The Exchange of Women and Male Homosexual Desire in Arthur Miller's *Death of a Salesman* and Lillian Hellman's *Another Part of the Forest*." Pp. 59–66 in *Feminist Readings of Modern American Drama*, ed. by June Schlueter. Rutherford, N.J.: Fairleigh Dickinson University Press, 1989.

Balakian, Jan. "Beyond the Male Locker Room: *Death of a Salesman* from a Feminist Perspective." Pp. 115–24 in *Approaches to Teaching Miller's Death of a Salesman*, ed. by Matthew C. Roudané. New York: The Modern Language Association of America, 1995.

Barker, Stephen. "The Crisis of Authenticity: *Death of a Salesman* and the Tragic Muse." Pp. 82–101 in *Approaches to Teaching Miller's Death of a Salesman*, ed. by Matthew C. Roudané. New York: The Modern Language Association of America, 1995.

Bentley, Eric. *The Playwright as Thinker: A Study of Drama in Modern Times*. New York: Meridian Books, 1963.

———. *In Search of Theater*. New York: Vintage Books, 1959.

Ben-Zvi, Linda. "'Home Sweet Home': Deconstructing the Masculine Myth of the Frontier in Modern Drama." Pp. 217–25 in *The Frontier Experience and the American Drama*, ed. by David Mogen, Mark Busby, and Paul Bryant. College Station: Texas A&M University Press, 1989.

Bettina, Sister M. "Willy Loman's Brother Ben: Tragic Insight in *Death of a Salesman*." Pp. 80–83 in *The Merrill Studies in Death of a Salesman. Comp. by Walter J. Meserve*. Columbus, Ohio: Charles E. Merrill, 1972.

Bhatia, Santosh K. *Arthur Miller: Social Drama as Tragedy*. New Delhi: Arnold-Heinemann, 1985.

Bierman, Judah, James Hart, and Stanley Johnson. "Arthur Miller: *Death of a Salesman*." Pp. 265–71 in *Arthur Miller: Death of a Salesman. Text and Criticism*, ed. by Gerald C. Weales. New York: Viking, 1967.

Bigsby, Christopher, ed. *Arthur Miller and Company*. London: Methuen Drama in association with The Arthur Miller Center for American Studies, 1990.

————, ed. *The Cambridge Companion to Arthur Miller*. Cambridge: Cambridge University Press, 1997.

————. *A Critical Introduction to Twentieth-Century American Drama 2: Tennessee Williams, Arthur Miller, Edward Albee*. Cambridge: Cambridge University Press, 1984.

————. "Introduction" to *Death of a Salesman: Certain Private Conversations in Two Acts and a Requiem*. New York: Penguin Books, 1998.

————. *Modern American Drama, 1945–1980*. New York: Cambridge University Press, 1992.

Billman, Carol. "Women and the Family in American Drama." *Arizona Quarterly 36*. 1 (1980): 35–49.

Bliquez, Guerin. "Linda's Role in *Death of a Salesman*." *Modern Drama* 10 (1968): 383–86.

Bloom, Harold, ed. *Willy Loman*. New York: Chelsea House, 1991.

Canning, Charlotte. "Is This Play About Women? A Feminist Reading of *Death of a Salesman*." Pp. 69–76 in *The Achievement of Arthur Miller: New Essays*, ed. by Steven R. Centola. Dallas: Contemporary Research Associates, 1995.

Centola, Steven R., ed. *The Achievement of Arthur Miller: New Essays*. Dallas: Contemporary Research Associates, 1995.

————. "'Just Looking for a Home': A Conversation with Arthur Miller." *American Drama* 1.1 (1991): 85–94.

Clark, Eleanor. "Old Glamour, New Gloom." *Partisan Review* 16 (1949): 631–35.

Cohn, Ruby. *Dialogue in American Drama*. Bloomington: Indiana University Press, 1971.

Corrigan, Robert W., ed. *Arthur Miller: A Collection of Critical Essays*. Englewood Cliffs, NJ: Prentice-Hall, 1969.

Couchman, Gordon W. "Arthur Miller's Tragedy of Babbitt." Pp. 68–75 in *The Merrill Studies in Death of a Salesman*. Comp. by Walter J. Meserve. Columbus, Ohio: Charles E. Merrill, 1972.

Demastes, William W. "Miller's Use and Modification of the Realistic Tradition." Pp. 74–81 in *Approaches to Teaching Miller's Death of a Salesman*, ed. by Matthew C. Roudané. New York: The Modern Language Association of America, 1995.

Di Giuseppe, Rita. "The Shadow of the Gods: Tragedy and Commitment in *Death of a Salesman*." *Quaderni di lingue e letterature* 14 (1989): 109–28.

Dillingham, William B. "Arthur Miller and the Loss of Conscience." Pp. 339–49 in *Arthur Miller: Death of a Salesman. Text and Criticism*, ed. by Gerald C. Weales. New York: Viking, 1967.

Driver, Tom F. "Strength and Weakness in Arthur Miller." Pp. 105–13 in *The Merrill Studies in Death of a Salesman*. Comp. by Walter J. Meserve. Columbus, Ohio: Charles E. Merrill, 1972.

Dukore, Bernard F. *Death of a Salesman and The Crucible: Text and Performance*. Atlantic Heights, N.J.: Humanities Press, 1989.

Eisinger, Chester E. "Focus on Arthur Miller's *Death of a Salesman*: The Wrong Dream." Pp. 165–74 in *American Dreams, American Nightmares*, ed. by David Madden. Carbondale and Edwardsville: Southern Illinois University Press, 1970.

Field, B. S., Jr. "Hamartia in *Death of a Salesman*." *Twentieth Century Literature* 18 (1972): 19–24.

Foster, Richard J. "Confusion and Tragedy: The Failure of Arthur Miller's *Death of a Salesman*." Pp. 82–88 in *Two Modern American Tragedies: Reviews and Criticism of Death of a Salesman and A Streetcar Named Desire*, ed. by John D. Hurrell. New York: Scribner's, 1961.

Goodman, Charlotte. "The Fox's Clubs: Lillian Hellman, Arthur Miller and Tennessee Williams." Pp. 130–42 in *Modern American Drama: The Female Canon*, ed. by June Schlueter. Rutherford, N.J.: Fairleigh Dickinson University Press, 1990.

Gordon, Lois. "*Death of a Salesman*: An Appreciation." Pp. 98–108 in *Twentieth Century Interpretations of Death of a Salesman*, ed. by Helene Koon. Englewood Cliffs, N.J.: Prentice-Hall, 1983.

Hagopian, John V. "Arthur Miller: The Salesman's Two Cases." *Modern Drama* 6 (1963): 117–25.

Harshbarger, Karl. *The Burning Jungle: An Analysis of Arthur Miller's Death of a Salesman*. Washington, D.C.: University Press of America, 1979.

Heilman, Robert Bechtold. *The Iceman, The Arsonist, and The Troubled Agent: Tragedy and Melodrama on the Modern Stage*. Seattle: University of Washington Press, 1973.

———. *Tragedy and Melodrama: Versions of Experience*. Seattle: University of Washington Press, 1968.

Hume, Beverly. "Linda Loman as 'The Woman' in Miller's *Death of a Salesman*." *NMAL; Notes on Modern American Literature* 9.3 (1985): Item 14.

Hurrell, John D., ed. *Two Modern American Tragedies: Reviews and Criticism of Death of a Salesman and A Streetcar Named Desire*. New York: Scribner's, 1961.

Hynes, Joseph A. "'Attention Must Be Paid....'" Pp. 280–89 in *Arthur Miller: Death of a Salesman. Text and Criticism*, ed. by Gerald C. Weales. New York: Viking, 1967.

Jackson, Esther Merle. "*Death of a Salesman*: Tragic Myth in the Modern Theatre." *CLA Journal* 7 (1963): 63–76.

Kintz, Linda. "The Sociosymbolic Work of Family in *Death of a Salesman*." Pp. 102–14 in *Approaches to Teaching Miller's Death of a Salesman*, ed. by Matthew C. Roudané. New York: The Modern Language Association of America, 1995.

Koenig, Rhoda. "Seduced by Salesman's Patter." *The [London] Sunday Times* 20 Oct. 1996: 10, 4.

Koon, Helene, ed. *Twentieth Century Interpretations of Death of a Salesman*. Englewood Cliffs, N.J.: Prentice-Hall, 1983.

Mandell, Jonathan. "Renaissance Man/At 82 Arthur Miller Is Pleasing a New Generation of Theatergoers." *Newsday* 28 Oct. 1997: B03.

Manders, John. *The Writer and Commitment*. Philadelphia: Dufour Editions, 1962.

Mason, Jeffrey D. "Paper Dolls: Melodrama and Sexual Politics in Arthur Miller's Early Plays." Pp. 103–15 in *Modern American Drama: The Female Canon*, ed. by June Schlueter. Rutherford, N.J.: Fairleigh Dickinson University Press, 1990.

Meserve, Walter J., compiler. *The Merrill Studies in Death of a Salesman*. Columbus, Ohio: Charles E. Merrill, 1972.

Miller, Arthur. *Conversations with Arthur Miller*, ed. by Matthew C. Roudané. Jackson: University Press of Mississippi, 1987.

———. *Death of a Salesman: Certain Private Conversations in Two Acts and a Requiem*. With an introduction by Christopher Bigsby. New York: Penguin, 1998.

———. *Salesman in Beijing*. New York: Viking, 1984.

———. *The Theater Essays of Arthur Miller*, ed. by Robert A. Martin and Steven R. Centola. Revised Edition. New York: Da Capo, 1996.

———. *Timebends: A Life*. New York: Penguin, 1995.

Morse, Donald. "The 'Life Lie' in Three Plays by O'Neill, Williams and Miller." Pp. 273–77 in *Cross-Cultural Studies: American, Canadian and European Literature: 1945–1985*, ed. by Mirko Jurak. Ljubljana, Yugoslavia: English Department, Filozofska Fakulteta, Edvard Kardelj University of Ljubljana, 1988.

Mottram, Eric. "Arthur Miller: The Development of a Political Dramatist in America."
Pp. 23–47 in *Arthur Miller: A Collection of Critical Essays*, ed. by Robert W. Corrigan.
Englewood Cliffs, N.J.: Prentice-Hall, 1969.

Murphy, Brenda. *Miller: Death of a Salesman*. Plays in Production Series. Cambridge:
Cambridge University Press, 1995.

Nathan, George Jean. "Review of *Death of a Salesman*." Pp. 279–85 in *The Theatre Book of
the Year, 1948–49*. New York: Knopf, 1949.

Nelson, Benjamin. *Arthur Miller: Portrait of a Playwright*. New York: David McKay, 1970.

O'Neill, Eugene. *Selected Letters*. Ed. by Travis Bogard and Jackson R. Bryer. New Haven,
Conn.: Yale University Press, 1988.

Otten, Charlotte F. "Who Am I? ... A Re-Investigation of Arthur Miller's *Death of a
Salesman*." Pp. 85–91 in *Twentieth Century Interpretations of Death of a Salesman*, ed.
by Helene Koon. Englewood Cliffs, N.J.: Prentice-Hall, 1983.

Parker, Brian. "Point of View in Arthur Miller's *Death of a Salesman*." Pp. 41–55 in
Twentieth Century Interpretations of Death of a Salesman, ed. by Helene Koon.
Englewood Cliffs, N.J.: Prentice-Hall, 1983.

Porter, Thomas E. *Myth and Modern American Drama*. Detroit: Wayne State University
Press, 1969.

Roudané, Matthew C., ed. *Approaches to Teaching Miller's Death of a Salesman*. New York:
The Modern Language Association of America, 1995.

———. "*Death of a Salesman* and the Poetics of Arthur Miller." Pp. 60–85 in *Arthur Miller
and Company*, ed. by Christopher Bigsby. London: Methuen Drama in association
with The Arthur Miller Center for American Studies, 1990.

Rowe, Kenneth Thorpe. *A Theater in Your Head*. New York: Funk & Wagnalls, 1960.

Savran, David. *Communists, Cowboys, and Queers: The Politics of Masculinity in the Work of
Arthur Miller and Tennessee Williams*. Minneapolis: University of Minnesota Press,
1992.

Schlueter, June, ed. *Feminist Readings of Modern American Drama*. Rutherford, N.J.:
Fairleigh Dickinson University Press, 1989.

———. "Re-membering Willy's Past: Introducing Postmodern Concerns through *Death
of a Salesman*." Pp. 142–54 in *Approaches to Teaching Miller's Death of a Salesman*, ed.
by Matthew Roudané. New York: The Modern Language Association of America,
1995.

Schlueter, June, and James K. Flanagan. *Arthur Miller*. New York: Ungar, 1987.

Schneider, Daniel E. *The Psychoanalyst and the Artist*. New York: International Universities
Press, 1950.

Shaw, George Bernard. "How to Write a Popular Play." In *Playwrights on Playwriting: The
Meaning and Making of Modern Drama from Ibsen to Ionesco*, ed. by Toby Cole. New
York: Hill & Wang, 1960.

Siegel, Paul N. "Willy Loman and King Lear." *College English* 17 (1956): 341–45.

Sievers, W. David. "Tennessee Williams and Arthur Miller." *Freud on Broadway: A History
of Psychoanalysis and the American Dream*. New York: Hermitage House, 1955.

Stanton, Kay. "Women and the American Dream of *Death of a Salesman*." Pp. 67–102 in
Feminist Readings of Modern American Drama, ed. by June Schlueter. Rutherford,
N.J.: Fairleigh Dickinson University Press, 1989.

Vogel, Dan. *The Three Masks of American Tragedy*. Baton Rouge: Louisiana State University
Press, 1974.

Weales, Gerald C. *American Drama since World War II*. New York: Harcourt, Brace &
World, 1962.

————, ed. *Arthur Miller: Death of a Salesman. Text and Criticism*. New York: Viking, 1967.

————. "Arthur Miller: Man and His Image." *Tulane Drama Review* 7.1 (1962): 165–80.

Welland, Dennis. *Miller the Playwright*. 3rd ed. New York: Methuen, 1985.

Whitley, Alvin. "Arthur Miller: An Attempt at Modern Tragedy." *Transactions of the Wisconsin Academy of Science, Arts, and Literature* 42 (1953): 257–62.

Williams, Raymond. *Modern Tragedy*. Stanford, Cal.: Stanford University Press, 1966.

Zeineddine, Nada. *Because It Is My Name: Problems of Identity Experienced by Women, Artists, and Breadwinners in the Plays of Henrik Ibsen, Tennessee Williams, and Arthur Miller*. Brauton Devon: Merlin Books, 1991.

FRED RIBKOFF

Shame, Guilt, Empathy, and the Search for Identity in *Arthur Miller's* Death of a Salesman

Among other things, tragedy dramatizes identity crises. At the root of such crises lie feelings of shame. You might ask: what about guilt? There is no question that guilt plays a major role in tragedy, but tragedy also dramatizes the way in which feelings of shame shape an individual's sense of identity, and thus propel him or her into wrongdoing and guilt. In fact, Bernard Williams examines the relation and distinction between shame and guilt in his study of ancient Greek tragedy and ethics, *Shame and Necessity*. He "claim[s] that if we can come to understand the ethical concepts of the Greeks, we shall recognise them in ourselves."[1] In the process of establishing a kinship between the Greeks and ourselves, Williams provides an excellent foundation upon which to build an argument on the dynamics of shame, guilt, empathy, and the search for identity in Arthur Miller's modern tragedy *Death of a Salesman*. Williams states that

> We can feel both guilt and shame towards the same action. In a moment of cowardice, we let someone down; we feel guilty because we have let them down, ashamed because we have contemptibly fallen short of what we might have hoped of ourselves....

From *Modern Drama* 43, no. 1 (Spring 2000): 48-55. © 2000 University of Toronto.

> ... It [guilt] can direct one towards those who have been
> wronged or damaged, and demand reparation in the name,
> simply, of what has happened to them. But it cannot by itself
> help one to understand one's relations to those happenings, or
> to rebuild the self that has done these things and the world in
> which that self has to live. Only shame can do that, because it
> embodies conceptions of what one is and of how one is related
> to others.[2]

In order to understand the identity crises of Miller's tragic characters in
Death of a Salesman, and especially the late, climatic scene in which Biff
confronts Willy with the truth, it is necessary to understand shame's relation
to guilt and identity. It is the confrontation with feelings of shame that
enables Biff to find himself, separate his sense of identity from that of his
father, and empathize with his father. Moreover, it is the denial of such
feelings that cripples Willy and the rest of the Loman family.

Until Biff stops to examine who he is, while in the process of stealing
the fountain pen of his old boss, Bill Oliver, feelings of shame determine his
self-perception as well as his conduct. Even before discovering his father
with "The Woman" in Boston, Biff's sense of self-worth, like that of his
brother Happy, is dependent on his father's conception of success and
manhood and on his father's approval. In fact, because Willy is abandoned at
the age of three by his father, his elder brother, Ben, becomes the measure of
success and manhood for his sons to live up to. Ben is, in Willy's own words,
"a great man!" "the only man I ever met who knew the answers."[3] "That's
just the way I'm bringing them up, Ben—rugged, well liked, all-around," says
Willy while reliving Ben's visit in the past (49). Early in the play, we see Biff
through the proud memory of his father. Willy asks Biff, "Bernard is not well
liked, is he?" and Biff replies, "He's liked, but he's not well liked" (33). Biff
inherits from his father an extremely fragile sense of self-worth dependent on
the perceptions of others. "Be liked and you will never want," says the proud
father of two sons who are, in his own words, "both built like Adonises" (33).
But according to the true Loman heroic creed, it is not good enough simply
to be "liked." As Willy points out to Happy earlier, "Charley is ... liked, but
he's not—well liked" (30).

Shame, together with the sense of inadequacy and inferiority manifest
in the need to prove oneself to others, is evident in both Loman sons, and of
course, in the fatherless father, Willy. The Loman men's shame propels them
into wrongdoing and guilt.[4] In Act One, Willy begs Ben to stay "a few days"
more, and, in the process of doing so, reveals the degree to which he feels
incomplete and inadequate:

WILLY, *longingly*: Can't you stay a few days? You're just what I need, Ben, because I—I have a fine position here, but I—well, Dad left when I was such a baby and I never had a chance to talk to him and I still feel—kind of temporary about myself. (51)

The fact that Willy feels "kind of temporary about" himself is reflected in his inability to complete a thought after he has raised the issue of his identity—the "I." This confession is riddled with dashes—or, in other words, uncomfortable, self-conscious pauses. While in the presence of his god-like brother, Ben, Willy, out of shame, constantly attempts to cover up the sense of failure and inferiority that threatens to expose his sense of inadequacy and weakness every time he is about to say what the "I" really feels.

Willy is driven to commit his greatest wrong by feelings of shame that arise out of his sense of inadequacy as a man. His adulterous affair with "The Woman" in Boston, which haunts both him and his son Biff, is a desperate attempt to confirm and maintain his self-esteem.[5] In the middle of Act One, while reliving the past, Willy confesses to his wife that "people don't seem to take to me" (36), that he "talk[s] too much. A man oughta come in with a few words. One thing about Charley. He's a man of few words, and they respect him" (37). After this confession. "The Woman" appears "*behind a scrim*" as his feelings of guilt for betraying his wife surface in his words to her. Just prior to "The Woman's" first spoken words and interruption, Willy attempts to make sense of his betrayal without mentioning it:

WILLY, *with great feeling*: You're the best there is, Linda, you're a pal, you know that? On the road—on the road I want to grab you sometimes and just kiss the life outa you. (38)

"*The Woman has come from behind the scrim [...] laughing,*" and Willy continues:

'Cause I get so lonely—especially when business is bad and there's nobody to talk to. I get the feeling that I'll never sell anything again, that I won't make a living for you, or a business, a business for the boys. (38)

Willy believes that he turns to another woman out of loneliness for his wife, Linda. But at the root of his loneliness and his need of a woman are feelings of shame he cannot face. He is driven by feelings of inadequacy and failure to seek himself outside of himself, in the eyes of others. "The Woman" makes him feel that he is an important salesman and a powerful man. After she interrupts Willy with the words, "I picked you," Willy immediately asks, "*pleased,*" "You picked me?" (38). Again, on the same page, after she says, "And I think you're a wonderful man." Willy asks, "You picked me, heh?" (38). Just prior to leaving, "The Woman" makes a point of saying exactly what Willy wants to hear. "I'll put you right through to the buyers," she says, and, feeling full of masculine power, "*slapping her bottom,*" Willy responds, "Right. Well, bottoms up!" (39).

The father's bravado is the son's shame. At the root of Biff's wrongdoing and feelings of guilt lie shame and feelings of inadequacy and inferiority. But, unlike his father, he faces, and learns from, his shame. Consequently, the play suggests that he can rebuild his sense of self-worth and re-establish his relation to others on healthier grounds. He makes sense of his guilt by confronting the shame buried deep in his sense of identity. Ultimately, the ability to do so enables him to empathize with his father.

Biff's inherited sense of inadequacy and inferiority send him "running home" (22) in springtime from the outdoor life out West—a life that reflects his own desires and needs. And yet, it is his father's wrong, a shameful act of adultery, coupled with Biff's failure to pass math and go to university to become a football star (as he and his father had hoped), that shatters Biff's already fragile sense of identity and sends him out West in the first place. His own desires and needs cannot hold him still. He is plagued by his father's, and his society's, measure of a person—the mighty dollar, the dream of "building a future" (22). Until Biff discovers his father with "The Woman" in Boston, Willy is as good as a god to him. So, rather than expose his father's shame, which, at some level, he experiences as his own, Biff runs, and attempts to hide, from the collapse of the ideal, invulnerable, infallible image of his father. Thus the source of his sense of identity in shame goes unquestioned. He continues to steal and to move from job to job, not so much because he feels guilty but because he feels ashamed of himself for not living up to an image of success that has already been proven to be a "fake." After he witnesses his father give "The Woman" in Boston "Mama's stockings!" Biff calls his father a "liar!" a "fake!" and a "phony little fake!" (121). He does not, however, reconcile this image of his father with his sense of himself. Not, that is, until he is in the process of stealing a fountain pen belonging his old boss, Bill Oliver. As he says to his father, "I stopped in the middle of that building and I saw—the sky" (132)—the same sky that is obscured from view by the "*towering, angular shapes* [...] *surrounding*" the Loman home "*on all sides*" (11), and which also forms part of the "inspiring" outdoor world Biff has left behind (22). Biff goes to see Oliver in a futile attempt to fit his, if you will, circular self into an "angular" world—a world in the process of crushing both the son and the father, men far more adept at using their hands than at using a pen. Biff reveals to his father that he has taken Oliver's pen, and that he cannot face Oliver again, but Willy accuses him of not "want[ing] to be anything," and Biff, *"now angry at Willy for not crediting his sympathy,"* exclaims, "Don't take it that way! You think it was easy walking into that office after what I'd done to him? A team of horses couldn't have dragged me back to Bill Oliver!" (112–13). There is no question that Biff feels guilty for what he has "done to" Oliver, first, by stealing "that carton of basketballs" (26) years ago, and second, by stealing his fountain pen. On the other hand, he also feels extremely ashamed of himself.

Biff's inherited sense of shame drives him to steal and to perform for his father. The fact that he steals does not, however, bother his father too much. Guilt can be concealed and, perhaps, forgiven and forgotten. Willy suggests as much when he advises Biff to say to Oliver: "You were doing a crossword puzzle and accidentally used his pen!" (112). But Biff's sense of himself is at stake, and he knows it. He knows that he cannot bear to be seen (the classic sign of shame) by Oliver. He can no longer separate his sense of himself from the act of stealing. Biff says to his father. "I stole myself out of every good job since high school!" (131). But, in essence, as Biff now realizes, his self was stolen by his inherited, shame-ridden sense of identity. He never had a chance to see himself outside his father's point of view. Willy feels attacked by Biff's confession that he "stole" himself "out of every good job," and responds: "And whose fault is that?" Biff continues: "And I never got anywhere because you blew me so full of hot air I could never stand taking orders from anybody! That's whose fault it is!" (131).

Biff understands his relation to others, notably his father, only after he literally goes unnoticed and unidentified by someone he thought would recognize him: Bill Oliver. Biff comes to the realization that there is no reason why Oliver should have recognized him, given that he couldn't recognize himself. That is, as Biff says to Happy, "I even believed myself that I'd been a salesman for him! And then he gave me one look and—I realized what a ridiculous lie my whole life has been! We've been talking in a dream for fifteen years. I was a shipping clerk" (104). Unlike his father's true self, which is immersed in shame and guilt, Biff's self surfaces and stays afloat because he learns about his guilt from his shame.

Willy's insistence that Biff is "spiting" him by not going to see Oliver prompts Biff to voice what he sees as the meaning behind his theft and his inability to face his old boss again: "I'm no good, can't you see what I am?" (113). In this case, it is not simply Biff's wrongdoing that makes him identify himself as "no good"; he has now grasped the fact that behind his habit of breaking the law lie feelings of shame. This question, "can't you see what I am?" represents the beginnings of Biff's separation of his own identity from that of his father. By the end of Act Two, Biff is certain, as he says to his brother, that "[t]he man don't know who we are!" At this point he is determined to force his father to "hear the truth—what you are and what I am!" (131, 130). He knows who he thought he was and, thus, why he stole Oliver's pen. As he reveals to his whole family,

> I stopped in the middle of that building and I saw—the sky. I saw the things that I love in this world. The work and the food and time to sit and smoke. And I looked at the pen and said to myself, what the hell am I grabbing this for? Why am I trying to become what I don't want to be? What am I doing in an office, making a contemptuous, begging fool of myself, when all I want is out there, waiting for me the minute I say I know who I am! Why can't I say that, Willy? *He tries to make Willy face him, but Willy pulls away and moves to the left.* (132)

"Willy," the father who has been transformed from "Dad" into simply a man in his son's eyes, cannot bear to have his dreams, and his heroic vision of his son, himself, and his own brother and father—the vision by which he lives and dies—exposed. Therefore, he *"pulls away"* in shame, before standing his ground and yelling, *"with hatred, threateningly,"* "The door of your life is wide open!" (132). Unlike the scene in the restaurant, in which Biff presents Happy with *"the rolled-up hose"* with which Willy intends to commit suicide and tells his brother that he "can't bear to look at his [father's] face!" out of shame (115), this time Biff does not turn away from his father. He insists on the truth being truly heard by his father. It is only after he realizes that this is an impossibility that *"he pulls away"* (133): "There's no spite in it any more. I'm just what I am, that's all" (133), says the son to his father. He now knows that he is "nothing" only under the umbrella of his father's destructive vision.

By the end of Act Two, Biff has a relatively clear understanding of who he is or, at the very least, who he is not. "I am not a leader of men," he says to his father in a *"fury,"* before *"he breaks down, sobbing"* (132–33). But his father cannot empathize with him because he is incapable of facing his own feelings of guilt and shame. To Willy, Biff's tears symbolize simply his son's love, and not, in any way, the struggle to separate from him. Biff demonstrates that he does in fact love his father, but, at the same time, this love is balanced by the recognition that if there is any chance of saving himself and his father he must leave home for good. The complexity of his feelings for his father goes unrecognized, however. Willy's response to Biff's breakdown is, "Oh, Biff! *Staring wildly*: He cried! Cried to me. *He is choking with his love, and now cries out his promise*: That boy—that boy is going to be magnificent!" (133).

What Biff wants from his father he ends up giving, without getting it back. He wants not only love, but empathy. Moreover, after confronting his own shame and discovering who he is not—that is, not the "boy" his father believes him to be—Biff demonstrates his ability to separate from his father and, consequently, his ability to empathize with him. In his dictionary of psychoanalysis, Charles Rycroft defines empathy as "[t]he capacity to put oneself into the other's shoes. The concept implies that one is both feeling oneself into the object and remaining aware of one's own identity as another person."[6] Biff does exactly this. In tears, he asks his father, "Will you let me go, for Christ's sake? Will you take that phony dream and burn it before something happens?" (133). He is not simply asking for his own freedom from the shame produced by not living up to the dream of success and being "well liked"; he is asking for his father's freedom from shame and guilt as well. He feels for his father and recognizes how "that phony dream" tortures him, at the same time that he retains his own sense of identity. But nothing can save Willy from his inability to accept the failure to live up to his own expectations—not even his son's empathy and forgiveness. Both are powerless in the face of shame.

In "Requiem," the final moments of Miller's tragedy, Biff is alone in his empathic understanding. Even Charley does not understand the meaning of Biff's final words about his father. "He had the wrong dreams. All, all, wrong. [...] He never knew who he was" (138, intervening dialogue omitted). Happy is *"ready to fight"* after these words, and Charley responds by saying to Biff, "Nobody dast blame this man. You don't understand: Willy was a salesman." But, as Linda suggests prior to this statement by Charley, "He was so wonderful with his hands," and it is this very suggestion that triggers Biff's final words about his father (138). Willy Loman was more himself, relatively free of guilt and shame, when he worked with his hands than at any other time in his life.

Driven by shame, he kills himself in order to preserve his dream of being "well liked" and a successful father and salesman. Of course, the irony is that because of his suicide the odds are very good that neither of his sons will benefit from his sacrifice, and nobody from his world of sales comes to his funeral. Linda's words at the end of the play, and especially the words, "We're free and clear" (139), reveal the degree to which she and her husband lived in denial, in fear of exposing the man who hid in shame behind the idea of being a successful salesman and father. To be "free and clear" is, ultimately, an impossibility for Willy Loman. His vision of success perpetuates crippling feelings of inferiority and inadequacy that drive him to destroy himself.

Unlike Biff, Willy does not confront and come to terms with his shame, and therefore he can never understand his guilt, nor his son's pain and his own responsibility for it. In "Tragedy and the Common Man," Miller states that "In [tragedies], and in them alone, lies the belief—optimistic, if you will, in the perfectibility of man."[7] In *Death of a Salesman*, he suggests, perhaps unintentionally, that the path to "perfection" lies in a confrontation with feelings of shame that enable one to understand guilt and arrive at a clearer sense of identity, as well as to empathize with others.

NOTES

1. Bernard Williams, *Shame and Necessity* (Berkeley and Los Angeles: U of California P, 1993), 10.

2. Ibid., 92–94.

3. Arthur Miller, *Death of a Salesman: Certain Private Conversations and a Requiem* (New York: Penguin, 1987), 48, 45. Subsequent references appear parenthetically in the text.

4. In addition to *Shame and Necessity*, Helen Merrell Lynd's *On Shame and the Search for Identity* has been influential in shaping my understanding of the distinction and relation between guilt and shame. Lynd states that "[a] sense of guilt arises from a feeling of wrongdoing, a sense of shame from a feeling of inferiority. Inferiority feelings in shame are rooted in a deeper conflict in the personality than the sense of wrongdoing in guilt." Helen Merrell Lynd, *On Shame and the Search for Identity* (New York: Harcourt, 1967), 22.

5. In *On Shame and the Search for Identity*, Lynd defines shame as "a wound to one's self-esteem, a painful feeling or sense of degradation excited by the consciousness of having done something unworthy of one's previous idea of one's own excellence" (23–24). See note 4.

6. Charles Rycroft, *A Critical Dictionary of Psychoanalysis* (London: Penguin 1988). 42.

7. Arthur Miller, "Tragedy and the Common Man," in *The Theater Essays of Arthur Miller*, ed. Robert A. Martin (New York: Viking, 1978), 7.

AUSTIN E. QUIGLEY

Setting the Scene:
Death of a Salesman *and* After the Fall

In his essay "*After the Fall* and After," Albert Wertheim makes a strong case for a decisive shift in Miller's career during the eight-year hiatus between the opening of his revised version of *A View from the Bridge* and the opening of *After the Fall* (1964). The latter, he suggests, in spite of an unenthusiastic critical response, marks the beginning of "the second flowering of Arthur Miller's playwriting career."[1] "Comparisons with Miller's earlier dramatic works can serve to cloud the discussion," he argues, and there is certainly some clarity to be gained by situating *After the Fall* largely in the context of the plays that succeed it.[2] But he also notes, in passing, Gerald Weales's remark that "*The Inside of His Head*, Miller's original title for *Death of a Salesman*, might well be an alternate title for *After the Fall*.... Since [the play] aptly locates its episodes within the convolutions of Quentin's brain, this is made manifest on-stage through the use of free-form sculpted areas" in which the various scenes are situated.[3]

As *Death of a Salesman* was written fifteen years before *After the Fall*, the continuity in Miller's writing career might be every bit as important as the discontinuities, and a more detailed comparison of the two plays confirms this to be the case. Even the evident contrasts between the two plays suggest not so much the differences between mutually exclusive alternatives, such as those provided when we contrast "open" with "closed," but the kind that

From *Arthur Miller's America: Theater & Culture in a Time of Change*, edited by Enoch Brater. © 2005 by the University of Michigan.

distinguish mutually implicating oppositions, like those of the two sides of a coin.[4]

It is in these respects that *Death of a Salesman* and *After the Fall* can shed some illumination not only on each other but also on the more general nature of Miller's dramatic work. It is in terms of structure and setting that the complementary function of the two plays becomes most clearly apparent. Their episodic configurations provide related settings for characters wrestling with issues at the outer limits of human experience; they also provide related problems for audiences seeking to grasp precisely what is at stake.

Structurally, both plays interweave scenes of the past and present, depicting events in a sequence at odds with their chronological progression. The most obvious consequences of this departure from a linear chronological structure become evident if we recall the characteristic structure of the well-made play, with its linear structural pattern of exposition, complication, crisis and resolution. In such a structure the crisis scene, coming late in the narrative, is one capable of redirecting the drama by enacting or reporting a decisive causal event for which someone is clearly responsible. In effect, chronology, linearity, causality and responsibility are aligned with each other along a single axis, and the work of the audience is correspondingly simple. But the equivalent scene in *Death of a Salesman* is the eventual dramatization, late in act 2, of the frequently signaled event in Boston that occurred when Biff, aged seventeen, discovered his father with a woman in a hotel room. But this is not a new event that turns the action in a new direction, nor is it a newly revealed event for any of the characters, as Willy and Biff already know of it and neither Linda nor Happy learns about it when it is finally dramatized on stage. Its causal status is thus rendered problematic by its structural deployment, and even more problematic if we ask ourselves about its thematic implications. Was Willy simply the victim of some bad timing and, without this chance encounter, would all otherwise have been well, or at least tolerable, for Willy, Biff and the rest of the family?

Causality, in fact, is one of the most problematic features of *Death of a Salesman*. The key problem is not the shortage of causal factors but their sheer number and variety, so much so that the play, with its episodic structure, has at times been criticized for failing to make them cohere. At various points in the play, Willy's radical discontentment is explicitly linked to a variety of causes: the rootlessness and alienation of an urban rather than rural way of life (stage set, 11; Ben, 85; Biff and Happy, 22–23, 61; Willy, 122); the growing population with consequently increased competition and reduced space (Willy, 17–18); the changing values of American society (Willy, 81); the underlying economic system (Happy, 24–25); the early loss of a guiding father figure (Willy, 51); Willy's failure as a husband (Willy,

107); his failure as a father (Willy, 93); his failure as a salesman (Willy, 37); his old age (Linda, 57); his lack of self-knowledge (Biff, 138); his misguided ambitions (Charley, 89); his excessive self-pity (Biff, 56); his unimpressive appearance (Willy, 37); and so on.[5] This diffusion of the causes of Willy's disenchantment with his life can invite us to dismiss the play as one depicting a disgruntled failure, full of hot air and foolish dreams, whose frequent complaints and evident limitations fail to converge into any coherent pattern. The episodic nature of the play, in these terms, serves more to conceal than clarify the implicit structure of the action.

The counterargument, however, is that Willy is, as Biff defiantly asserts, "a dime a dozen" (132) in every respect except the one that Biff cannot quite comprehend: his desire and determination not to be. The diversity of negative evidence and hostile circumstances then serves not so much to muddy the thematic waters as to clarify the scale of Willy's determination to hold onto an aspiration in the face of counter-evidence of every imaginable kind.

And it is here that the actions of the leading characters need to be carefully integrated into the setting and structure of the play. The episodic material consists of three major kinds: events in the present that repeatedly reconfirm Willy's limitations; events in the past clarifying the status of the encounter in the Boston hotel room in establishing Willy as a fraud; and events in the past that promise another through-line for the play, one that validates Willy's aspiration to have lived a life that counts for something significant. The battle among the characters to establish which will be the defining moment in the narrative, Willy's firing (83), Willy and Biff's encounter in Boston (117) or Biff's performance at Ebbets Field (68), is a battle whose significance hinges surprisingly not on Willy's capacity to deceive himself, but on his inability to deceive himself enough. And this is one of the ways in which the play offers more than any of the characters ever manages to grasp.

The weight and variety of the negative evidence that Willy is unable to evade or ignore, in effect, lend cumulative stature to his unyielding determination to counter that evidence by transcending his constraining circumstances. The strength of this determination is reinforced rather than diminished by Willy's explicit recognition of the desperate strategies to which he resorts to keep the hope alive. Faced with the lowest point in his life and career, Willy acknowledges the strategies of deception and self-deception required to keep his mammoth aspirations alive for himself and his family, in spite of his limitations and theirs:

Willy: I was fired today.... I was fired, and I'm looking for a little
good news to tell your mother, because the woman has

> waited and the woman has suffered. The gist of it is that I
> haven't got a story left in my head, Biff. So don't give me a
> lecture about facts and aspects. I am not interested. Now
> what've you got to say to me? (107)

The direct appeal to Biff to provide him with an enabling story rather than
with disabling facts is continuous with a disposition to live on the promise,
of future achievements—achievements that might ratify the family's
strengths and minimize their moments of disillusionment. But the promising
stories of future achievement are not themselves enough, either to satisfy
Willy or to create so powerful a play.

If the encouraging stories Willy collects and invokes to ratify his
preferred narrative line involved mere escapism and self-deception, this
would be a less significant play. But there is a reality principle at issue here
that is fundamental to the play and to Miller's work as a whole. Though it
would be difficult to defend Willy against accusations of self-deception, the
self-deception is as much strategic as self-indulgent. The solution Biff offers
to their problems, self-knowledge based on external evaluation, is thus
illuminatingly inadequate:

> *Biff*: What am I doing in an office, making a contemptuous,
> begging fool of myself, when all I want is out there, waiting
> for me the minute I say I know who I am.... I am not a
> leader of men, Willy, and neither are you. You were never
> anything but a hard-working drummer who landed in the
> ash can like all the rest of them! I'm one dollar an hour,
> Willy. I tried seven states and couldn't raise it. A buck an
> hour! Do you gather my meaning? I'm not bringing home
> any prizes any more, and you're going to stop waiting for
> me to bring them home! (132)

Biff's claim that in self-knowledge lies satisfaction is countered, of course, by
the vehemence of Willy's "I am not a dime a dozen! I am Willy Loman, and
you are Biff Loman!" (132), by the life he has lived to keep Biff's debilitating
evaluation at bay, and by the death he deploys as a culminating effort to
restart the cycle of success for himself and for Biff. And the trouble with
Biff's version of self-knowledge is that it is based upon external evaluations
that do not include internal values and personal aspirations, which have their
own reality claims.

In a world in which everyone grows and changes, the challenge the play
presents is one of requiring us to decide when aspirations are unrealistic

and/or unworthy. Aspiration, after all, must often lead achievement into being, otherwise new achievements and new achievers would emerge only by chance. Lurking in the background of Biff's remark that Willy had the wrong dreams (138) and of Charley's remark that "a salesman has got to dream, boy" (138) is that characteristic notion of an American dream in which personal and social transformation is a widely shared expectation, an expectation ratified in a great many rags-to-riches stories of the kind exemplified by the career of Willy's brother, Ben. But if aspiration is an enabling aspect of achievement, who is to say when aspiration, necessarily at odds with current reality, is excessive? And the play's episodic structure and competing narrative lines suspend the question in the action along with others it invites the audience to consider.

It is in the play's epilogue that the overall function of the play's episodic structure becomes most clearly apparent, and it is very much one of challenging the audience to locate the appropriate means of measuring Willy's worth. It is evident enough in the play's action that Willy has many failings, is often self-deceived and self-deceiving, and is much misguided about what might constitute worthwhile success. But those limitations provide neither the measure of the man nor the measure of the play. What the epilogue provides to supplement the three stories that have obsessed Willy, one ratified by his firing, another by the event in Boston, and the other by the event at Ebbets Field, are the stories each of the other characters derives from the action and the values each locates in them. For Linda, Willy was a success after all, as he had paid off the mortgage; for Charley, the career of salesman was a destructive choice, and his raising of Bernard to be a bookworm and a within-the-system success exemplifies a set of values different from Willy's; for Happy, the way forward is beating the system by playing with rather than by the rules and doing so better than anyone else; and, as we have seen, for Biff it is a matter of reducing expectations to one aspect of self-knowledge. But the final speech is Linda's, as she both asserts and questions a mode of measuring Willy's value that has sustained her commitment to him, despite all his evident failings:

Linda: Forgive me, dear. I can't cry. I don't know what it is, but I can't cry. I don't understand it. Why did you ever do that? ... Why did you do it? I search and search and I search, and I can't understand it, Willy. I made the last payment on the house today. Today, dear. And there'll be nobody home. (*A sob rises in her throat.*) We're free and clear. (*Sobbing more fully, released.*) We're free. (*Biff comes slowly toward her.*) We're free.... We're free ... (139)

And, at this point, *"the apartment buildings rise into sharp focus"* (139), reminding us at the end of the play, as they did at the beginning, of the sense of confinement and containment that the realistic aspects of the set provide to Linda's notions of freedom and success and to Willy's larger hopes and aspirations.

The action of the epilogue, however, takes place on the apron at the front of the stage, and the scene is not one circumscribed by the realism of the set: In "clothes of mourning" and accompanied by the beat of "a dead march," the characters "move toward the audience, through the wall-line of the kitchen" and out to "the limit of the apron" (136). And there, closest to the audience, and removed from the realistic set, the characters debate questions of sufficiency and excess:

> *Linda*: I can't understand it. At this time especially. First time in
> thirty-five years we were just about free and clear. He only
> needed a little salary. He was even finished with the dentist.
> *Charley*: No man only needs a little salary. (137)

Linda's domestic dreams seem impoverished when compared to Willy's implausible but more grandiose designs. Charley's remark, however, serves not only to raise the question of how much salary should suffice but also how much achievement, recognition, admiration, love, enduring impact and so on should suffice.

Willy's strength and weakness is his inability to locate a satisfactory measure of sufficient achievement, and he died, as he lived, fatally attracted to the notion that happiness consists of endless expectation of better things on the horizon. As Happy puts it: "Dad is never so happy as when he's looking forward to something!" (105). Willy's sense of containment and confinement is all-pervasive, and the "boxed in" neighborhood provides only an example and not a basic cause of his frustration. His preferred narrative line reaches beyond these constraints, and the play's structure and setting follow suit. When the play extends its episodic structure into a stage set whose partial transparency is designed to move the action beyond representational chronology to presentational rearrangement, it opens access to a world beyond the walls, a realm in which the possibilities of action, measurement and value extend beyond anything that the characters and their sociohistorical situation can encompass.

The play begins, as the stage direction puts it, with a melody, played upon a flute, that tells of "grass and trees and the horizon" (11). Much has been made of the grass and trees, but it is to the horizon that the episodic action of the play ultimately directs our attention. When Willy dies, there is no consensus on the stage about how we should measure his strengths and limitations or the ultimate value of the obsessive aspirations for which he is prepared to sacrifice his life. The conversation in the epilogue emerges from the realistic set of the play out onto the apron of the stage and ultimately out into the auditorium, where it will then be extended further. And looming ahead is a play of similarly episodic structure, that likewise seeks to entangle the audience in questions the play is better able to ask than answer; and in that play, too, questions about the appropriate limits of expectation, aspiration, responsibility and commitment play a central role. As Quentin puts it at a key point in the action: "If there's love, it should be limitless"— that play is, of course, *After the Fall*.[6]

Some of the issues that are central to the action of *Death of a Salesman* recur explicitly in *After the Fall*. Quentin asks himself a question that might well have been put to Biff: "Maybe it's not enough—to know yourself. Or maybe it's too much" (58). Too much, he suggests, because "the truth, after all, may merely be murderous. The truth killed Lou, destroyed Mickey" (61). But if the truth is not a reliable guide; what is the alternative? Which priorities should have precedence and how do we decide? As Quentin puts it in resigning from his law firm: "I couldn't concentrate on a case anymore.... I felt I was merely in the service of my own success" (2)—a self-criticism that Willy might well have contemplated at some point. And these thematic concerns, along with the episodic structures and fluid movements across time and place, link two otherwise radically contrasting plays. The two plays deal with significantly different aspects of human experience that turn out to be closely connected, the first play posing serious questions about the appropriate ceiling on belief and aspiration, the other about viable limits on doubt and despair.

For Quentin, as for Willy, a weight of evidence is cumulatively developed in an episodic structure from a variety of contexts and a range of examples. For Willy, the weight of evidence suggests that he is, indeed, a dime a dozen, and his manic/heroic response is to commit himself to a counter-narrative with his death as one of its central and enabling components. For Quentin, the weight of negative evidence raises a question of a different, but just as troubling kind, one that also requires of him an act of ratifying intervention.

Quentin's catalogue of exemplary instances includes the contemptuous criticism of his father by his mother, when, after many years of happy marriage, she calls him "an idiot" (20) for bungling the family finances; a complementary betrayal of the memory of the mother by the father when he registers and votes only two months after her death (10); Quentin's best friend's wife flirting provocatively with him (23); friends abandoning friends in the face of government investigations into un-American activities (33); Quentin's own "joy" when the suicide of his friend, Lou, relieves him of the obligation to defend him (59); the failure of his two marriages (42, 112); and his temporary abandonment as a small child by his parents (76). This selection of events seems so much skewed in the direction of pessimism and self-pity that it leaves the audience uncertain whether Quentin is deliberately seeking to ratify despair or struggling to come to terms with his own faults by focusing upon those of others. Willy, unlike Quentin, acknowledges both good and bad throughout, but Quentin seems obsessed with the bad. What restores the necessary balance to the play is Quentin's eventual question to himself: "Why is betrayal the only truth that sticks[?]" (76). And it is here, as was the case with *Death of a Salesman*, that it becomes essential to embed the actions of the characters in the context of the overall action of a play whose structure and setting play a central role.

The opening and closing scenes set the parameters of the inquiry Quentin is undertaking: "I have a bit of a decision to make," he announces at the outset to a "Listener" he has summoned to help him work it through (2). The decision involves whether or not to make a commitment to a new relationship with Holga when the weight of history, his own and other people's, seems to demonstrate that love between friends, siblings, spouses and other relatives promises more than it is ever able to deliver. His recurring bewilderment with "the death of love" (64) raises questions for Quentin not only about his own ability to love, but also about human bonds in general: "I don't know any more what people *are* to one another" (7), he asserts. "It's like some unseen web of connection between people is simply not there" (39). And it is in this context that the concentration camp tower that frames Holga's entry into the play (5) marks the ultimate extension of the collapse of human respect, responsibility, love and care that is exemplified in different ways in Quentin's catalogue of betrayals.

The answer to his question of why "betrayal is the only truth that sticks" emerges from his increasing awareness of the inappropriateness of the standards he invokes to establish the worth of personal commitments in general. Late in the play, the issue becomes both explicit in the dialogue and evident in the stage images:

> It's that if there is love, it must be limitless, a love not even of persons but blind, blind to insult, blind to the spear in the flesh, like justice blind, like ... *Felice appears behind him. He has been raising up his arms. Father appears, slumped in chair.*
> Mother's voice, *off*: Idiot! (100).

The tableau and the voice register the accumulating dramatic evidence of a counterargument to Quentin's views on the necessity for limitless love, a counterargument that has been evolving throughout the play. As he argues for the necessity that love be limitless, his arms move once more toward the iconic figure of crucifixion that has recurred in the play. His mother's repeatedly recalled condemnation of his father suddenly critiques, in this context, both the father in the past and the son in the present. As it does so, another narrative line begins to take precedence, one that, as in *Death of a Salesman*, evolves through the network of images, episodes and questions, one whose point of departure early in the action suggests a different way of configuring the material, weighing the evidence and setting standards of value: "Why do I think of things falling apart?" he asks. "Were they ever whole?" (26).

It is in their capacity to have their unfolding events reconfigured into differing narratives that the episodic structures of *Death of a Salesman* and *After the Fall* invite comparison. In both cases Miller promotes and controls this reconfiguration by deploying not just a sequence of nonchronological events but also a series of redefined relationships among images, events and issues. If *Death of a Salesman* invites us to ponder in these terms the appropriate means of validating aspiration, *After the Fall* invites us to join Quentin in pondering the appropriate means of validating despair. But in both cases there is more in the plays than the characters finally grasp. Betrayal is the only truth that sticks in Quentin's initial narrative because his mode of measurement generates expectations that set up everyone, including himself, for failure. The other narrative he begins to construct, the one that incorporates his recognition of "the lie of limitless love" (107), is one that emerges gradually in the episodic action. It arises in opposition to the narrative of universal betrayal that leads Quentin directly from domestic disappointments to concentration camp catastrophes. The second narrative recovers for Quentin some faith in the strength of personal commitments, and it does so by adjusting the scale upon which worthwhile achievement is measured. But just as in *Death of a Salesman*, the opposing narratives coexist, along with the indication that others might also be contemplated. Neither play settles all the issues it raises. The answers provided are very much answers offered by the characters rather than the answers of the plays. And in the case of *After the Fall*, this has large consequences for the way in which we conceive of its structure and function.

One of the key challenges in performing *After the Fall* is to achieve an appropriate balance between the two voices of Quentin, who serves as both character and narrator, and between those voices and the other "voices" of the play, including that of the set and its dramatic images. The opening stage directions are specific enough: "The action takes place in the mind, thought, and memory of Quentin.... The effect ... will be the surging, flitting, instantaneousness of a mind questing over its own surfaces and into its depths" (1). And it does so in the presence of a Listener who is invoked as a trusted friend and whose responses and advice will be taken seriously. Private concerns are being tested in a public context and, as the Listener is strategically located at the front of the auditorium, the theater audience is implicated in the role of trusted respondent. This, in turn, has its own effect on Quentin's role as stage narrator, enabling him to remain in character as a narrator addressing a Listener within the world of the play. The repeatedly signaled interrogative mode of narration is thus one that should result in shared inquiry into dramatized material, rather, than one in which the narrator is presumed to know best. Indeed the very notion of "best" is rendered problematic by the evolving action.

Quentin's question, "Why is betrayal the only truth that sticks[?]" is thus only one of many questions and queries that are raised by Quentin in the action, by Quentin about the action, or by events and images in the action. For example, "I don't know what I'd be bringing to that girl [Holga]" (5); "I don't understand why that girl [Felice] sticks in my mind" (11); "I don't know why this [concentration camp] hit me so" (12); "Why can't I mourn her [his mother]" (16); "Why do I make such stupid statements" (4); and the key questions: "Why do I think of things falling apart? Were they ever whole?" (26).

What makes the structures of his life, of the narrative he develops and of the play as a whole so mutually problematic is the explicit search for a governing principle that will give life a sense of wholeness, character a sense of governing purpose and individuals a shared sense of responsibility. As Quentin puts it early in the play:

> I've lost the sense of some absolute necessity. Whether I open a book or think of marrying again, it's so damned clear I'm choosing what I do—and it cuts the strings between my hands and heaven.... And I keep looking back to when there seemed to be some duty in the sky. I had a dinner table and a wife ... a child and the world so wonderfully threatened by injustices I was born to correct. It seemed so fine! Remember—when there were good people and bad people? And how easy it was to tell! The worst son of a bitch, if he loved Jews and hated Hitler, he was a buddy. (22)

The "choosing" that he now finds so repugnant seems to him like selecting options on the basis of personal preference and situational expediency rather than on the basis of more general principles. This sense of living a diminished life is set against an earlier experience, in the midst of world war, of a direct link between personal choice, human justice and moral consequence. The trouble with that nostalgia for a simpler world of simple moral choice is, of course, that it was never that simple, even though world war simplified some issues by pushing others temporarily to one side. The other trouble is that, by temporarily ratifying a world of simple moral choice, by reinforcing the claims of a moral world in which things were either fully good or fully bad, it helped establish for Quentin the narrative of universal standards and consequently of universal betrayal. In such a context, every failure of human relationship becomes, in effect, the same failure with the same ultimate consequence:

> *The tower lights*. Everything is one thing! *You* see—I don't know what we are to one another! ... It's like some unseen web of connection between people is simply not there. And I always relied on it, somehow. (33 and 39)

The judgmental absolutism of a simple moral universe serves to link domestic betrayals directly to concentration camp atrocities, for the lack of total trust between human beings is readily convertible into its absolute absence.

This is the narrative that has led Quentin to the brink of despair, but it is important to recognize that it is a narrative in the play and not the narrative of the play. From the outset Quentin persistently questions it. Indeed, the invitation to the Listener to hear him out is evidently prompted by a desire to find a way of saying "yes" to Holga, thus committing himself to a third marriage after the failure of his first two. Those who question the juxtaposition of domestic squabbles and concentration camp atrocities are right to do so, but wrong to fault the play for unquestioningly doing so. For what the play ambitiously seeks to establish is not just a rationale for such linkage, but also a plausible alternative narrative that will enable Quentin to transcend the first one. Just as important, however, is the effort to provide an alternative way of asking questions about the issues raised that leaves the audience evaluating, and not just assenting to, Quentin's answers to his own questions.

Quentin's second narrative, painfully salvaged from the wreckage of the first, is that we accept our own evil and live, that the concentration camp provides the outer limit of human failure, but not its characteristic scale or its inevitable destination.

> What burning cities taught her and the death of love taught me: that we are very dangerous! ... To know, and even happily, that we

meet unblessed: not in some garden of wax fruit and painted trees, that lie of Eden, but after, after the Fall, after many, many deaths. Is the knowing all? And the wish to kill is never killed, but with some gift of courage one may look into its face when it appears, and with a stroke of love—as to an idiot in the house— forgive it, again and again ... forever? (113–14)

This is Quentin's culminating "vision" (113), but it is not that of the play. The lines conclude with a question mark and are immediately followed by a stage direction indicating a question from the Listener, to whom Quentin responds not with conviction, but with continuing doubt:

He is evidently interrupted by the Listener.
Quentin: No, it's not certainty, I don't feel that. But it does seem feasible not to be afraid. Perhaps it's all one has. I'll tell her that.... Yes, she will, she'll know what I mean. (114)

It is Holga, of course, who introduced the image of the idiot child (22) to the play, and their narrative alternative to the one with which Quentin began seems only to have swung the pendulum of expectation from the "lie of limitless love," of excessive expectation, to the "truth" of limitless capacity to hate. In the context of that murderous human capacity, any kind or degree of selfless commitment is enhanced in value. The achievement of limited goals in such a context suffices to encourage the belief that even if things are not ideal, they are nevertheless tolerable, acceptable and perhaps worthy of celebration. The play concludes with Quentin and Holga expressing their mutual commitment with a minimal gesture of mutual recognition, each saying "Hello" to the other, with the evident implication that their relationship will continue. In the context of the narrative they have generated together, even so small a commitment is a reassuring achievement.

Once "limitless love" has been recognized as an excessive expectation, what follows from it is not what Quentin initially made of it—that limited love and a capacity for murder are only inches apart—but that the expectation itself was seriously misleading. It is not a matter of accepting that human beings are not capable of this ideal of commitment, but that the notion of that as an ideal is itself a mistaken one. And much of the action of the play lends itself to a recurring review of its status and to a sustained search for a viable alternative. And that search is invited as Quentin's is conducted—through differing interpretations of and alignments among the play's evocative episodes.

The fact that Quentin's readiness to defend Lou is at odds with his desire to be released from this unwelcome responsibility is something that could as easily be invoked to enhance the value of his readiness to defend him nevertheless, as invoked to diminish it. Louise's desire not to be "a praise machine" in her marriage to Quentin but to remain somehow "a separate person" (41) is not a desire that is invalidated by the failure of the marriage. And Quentin's father's capacity to register and vote after the death of his wife can lead to other conclusions than that he lacked sufficient commitment to the relationship. Indeed many of these images of qualified commitment invite comparison and contrast with an image of maternal love so absolute that Quentin is stunned to recognize it as somehow fraudulent, nevertheless.

> *Mother*: Darling, there is never a depression for great people! The first time I felt you move, I was standing on the beach at Rockaway ... And I saw a star, and it got bright, and brighter, and brighter! And suddenly it fell, like some great man had died, and you were being pulled out of me to take his place, and be a light, a light in the world!
> *Quentin, to Listener*: Why is there some ... air of treachery in that? (66–67)

The "praise machine" mother loving her son into her version of greatness is, indeed, unexpectedly treacherous, not least because it speaks of her needs and interests before she has listened to his. And in Quentin's initial narrative the thread of treachery in unqualified admiration is traced from one relationship to another. In Quentin's mind Felice, too, admired him for all the wrong reasons ("I feel like a mirror in which she somehow saw herself as glorious" [6]). And his dismay that he finds himself unable to grieve for his dead mother is phrased in terms similar enough to weave the two relationships together.

> *Mother appears on upper platform, arms crossed as in death*. I still hear her voice in the street sometimes, loud and real, calling me. And yet she's under the ground. That whole cemetery—I saw it like a field of buried mirrors in which the living merely saw themselves. I don't seem to know how to grieve for her. (6)

And all of these questions about separateness and union in loving relationships focus finally on the relationship that raises most graphically for Quentin the question of locating appropriate standards and expectations. The romance with Maggie emerges in the context of a failing marriage and the death of a mother whom he is finding difficult to mourn. And the play's images position Maggie at the pole opposite to his mother. Where the mother sought to love Quentin into an image that made her seem glorious, Maggie seeks to love Quentin in a glorious mold entirely of his own choosing:

> *Quentin*: You seem to think you owe people whatever they
>   demand!
> *Maggie*: I know. (83)

The ironic consequence of such unqualified commitment is, however, provided by the false name Maggie proposes to adopt if she were to visit him in Washington:

> *Maggie*: I could register in the hotel as Miss None.
> *Quentin*: N-u-n?
> *Maggie*: No—"n-o-n-e"—like nothing. I made it up once 'cause I
>   can never remember a fake name, so I just have to think of
>   nothing and that's me! *She laughs with joy.* (77)

In both relationships, an ideal of love that goes back to the Bible, that of two people becoming one, is depicted in terms that reveal its potential limitations. Situated between the two extremes is Louise's insistence that even in a marriage she must remain "a separate person" (41). But this is a claim that initially enrages Quentin:

> *Quentin*: When you've finally become a separate person, what the
>   hell is there?
> *Louise, with a certain unsteady pride*: Maturity.
> *Quentin*: I don't know what that means.
> *Louise*: It means that you know another person exists. (42)

Across this spectrum of separateness, connection and union, the action of the play positions its various episodes, with less than satisfactory results on all sides. But, as noted, personal satisfaction or even happiness is not the only thing at stake. The religious images and phrases that permeate both the play and its title focus repeatedly not just on what feels good, but on what is best, and best is a moral and not just an ethical and social context. And it is this recurring linkage of the personal and the moral that repeatedly escalates expectations of what a personal relationship should achieve and elevates the standards of measurement characters invoke.

What is at stake here for the play, as well as for Quentin, is the appropriate scale of consequence and implication for an individual life, a personal relationship and a species-wide sense of reciprocal responsibility. The word "moral" recurs repeatedly in the play, but most characteristically as a question whose accompanying assertion is rendered increasingly problematic:

> *Quentin*: What the hell is moral? And what am I, to even ask that
>   question? A man ought to know—a decent man knows that
>   like he knows his own face! (57)

The action of the play validates the first question more than the subsequent assertion. Brother Dan seemed to know exactly how right and wrong line up when he decided to devote his life to salvaging those of his parents, while Quentin moved away to build a life of his own. But whatever the virtues of Dan's choice, the action of the play suggests it is not the only good choice, though Quentin seems initially inclined to see it so. As he puts it in retrospect: "Yes, good men stay ... although they die there" (68). For Quentin, as for us, questions arise in these complicated choices about the limits of obligations to others, limits that fuel Quentin's fear that our capacity for independence can degenerate rapidly into indifference, an indifference that reaches its culmination in concentration camp catastrophe: "In whose name do you ever turn your back—*he looks out at the audience*—but in your own? In Quentin's name. Always in your own blood-covered name you turn your back!" (112).

In the absence of a governing moral standard, a fixed and final set of principles, the action of the play begins to exemplify an alternative source of standards, with its evolving set of complex images each effectively critiquing each other. What follows upon the recurring demonstration in the action— that a vocabulary of right and wrong will not suffice to accommodate the complexities of the episodes—is not an argument that anything can be situationally justified. The recurring images of the concentration camp render that position untenable. What emerges from the various episodes is the necessity for judgment even in the absence of a governing standard of value. While we may not know what is best for all people on all occasions, we incur the obligation, nevertheless, to recognize what are better choices than others in a variety of different contexts.

Rather than providing a single mode of measuring or a unified narrative establishing a single principle of value, the action of the play provides a variety of exemplary instances in which each effectively measures the other, and these complex examples are not convertible into a governing precept. The characteristically interrogative tone of the play does not move from question to answer but from a variety of questions to multiple modes of generating answers.

What the play offers, however, is not simply the multiplicity of relativistic perspectives. Rather it is, as the structure and setting of the play exemplify, the multiplicity of coherent configurations of episodes that will guide us for a while, before the further complexity of human experience requires us to supplement them and reconfigure them one more time. Quentin's development of a narrative alternative to the one with which he began is not the achievement of a final narrative. Experience may not finally teach us what is always best, but, suitably contemplated and interrogated, it can help us make informed but not infallible decisions about what is likely to be better, as we compare current situations to others both like and unlike them. The play's complex structure is one of juxtaposed memories leading to a present-time decision, and it is no accident that Holga is described in this context as an "archeologist" (3). The set's governing image and the play's governing structure are thus those of evolving historical multiplicity. And it is in this context that character is situated, moral choice exercised and commitments made.

Between the God-self, who creates people in his own image, and the nonself, content to be created in someone else's terms, lies the separate person who forms variable connections with others, not on the basis of a single decision totally and forever, but on the basis of recurring decisions about whether to continue and extend unfolding relationships. The total and forever commitment ultimately emerges from the play not as an unachievable ideal but as a mistaken ideal. The strength of Quentin and Holga's evolving relationship lies in its repeated renewal by people independent enough to be able to walk away but bonded enough to want to stay. Giving, in any relationship, requires givers, separable people whose giving acquires part of its value from their capacity not to give. The final shape of the relationship, its unfolded narrative, is thus not given in the initial episode of commitment; the end is not written into the beginning of either the relationship or the play. For this reason the play concludes with an exchanged "Hello," which promises but does not guarantee further renewal of commitment. Certainty does not replace doubt, and regular reconsideration and renewal are an essential part of the relationship we have witnessed and of any narrative it will eventually generate.

The episodic structure of the play and the scenic images of ever-renewed inquiry thus lead Quentin's audience, as *Death of a Salesman* led Willy's, to a position outside of any of the narratives generated or posited by the characters. With Willy exploring the viability of unlimited aspiration and

Quentin the validity of unlimited despair, the plays invite the audience to continue the inquiries beyond what the characters finally grasp, with episodic structures indicating that responsibilities, like causes, are never single or simple; those responsibilities remain unavoidable nevertheless. As Quentin puts it in characteristically interrogative fashion: "how else do you touch the world—except with a promise?" (61)—with a hypothetical narrative about what the future might hold. Such a narrative is informed by what the past has provided, but governed as much by a commitment to achieve more as by a readiness to settle for the less that has often been achieved in the past.

In the two plays neither Willy nor Quentin is able to locate an ultimately reliable mode of evaluating the claims of optimism and despair, but the plays provide, in their episodic structures and interacting images, the complexity of the experiential material we must draw upon and of the demands we make on it. In doing so they provide the word *moral*, in Miller's whole work, with a viability that enables his characters, though grounded in stage realism, to implicate and explore worlds that lie beyond what such realism can otherwise accommodate and contain. The complex structures and settings of these plays register and render characteristic concerns that arise in differing ways in many of Miller's plays: linking the social to the moral but relating morality to accountability rather than to predictability; positioning the linearity of narratives between episodic fragmentation and transformative reconfiguration; reconciling character reliability with personal aspiration and social change, achieved knowledge with continuing inquiry, barbarism with transcendence and realism with dimensions of experience it cannot readily accommodate. A creative interlocking of situation, set and structure gives the plays a power larger than character or conclusion can circumscribe, and audiences a role that continues after the curtain falls.

NOTES

1. Albert Wertheim, "Arthur Miller: *After the Fall* and After," in *Essays on Contemporary American Drama*, ed. Hedwig Bock and Albert Wertheim (Munich: M. Hueber, 1981), 19.

2. Wertheim, "Arthur Miller," 20.

3. Wertheim, "Arthur Miller," 20.

4. C. K. Ogden, *Opposition: A Linguistic and Psychological Analysis* (Bloomington: Indiana University Press, 1967).

5. Arthur Miller, *Death of a Salesman* (New York: Viking Press, 1971). All page references are to this edition.

6. Arthur Miller, *After the Fall* (New York: Viking Press, 1973). All page references are to this edition.

Afterthought

"A man can get anywhere in this country on the basis of being liked." Arthur Miller's remark, made in an interview, has a peculiar force in the context of American political and social history. One reflects upon Ronald Reagan, a president impossible (for me) either to admire or to dislike. Miller, despite his palpable literary and dramatic limitations, has a shrewd understanding of our country. *Death of Salesman* is now over half a century old, and retains its apparently perpetual relevance. The American ethos is sufficiently caught up by the play so that Miller's masterwork is clearly not just a period piece. If there is a legitimate tragic drama by an American author, then it must be *Death of a Salesman*.

Family romances almost invariably are melodramatic; to convert them to tragedy, you need to be the Shakespeare of *King Lear*, or at least of *Coriolanus*. Miller has a fondness for comparing *Death of a Salesman* to *King Lear*, a contrast that itself is catastrophic for Miller's play. Ibsen, at his strongest, can sustain some limited comparison to aspects of Shakespeare, but Miller cannot. Like Lear, Willy Loman needs and wants more familial love than anyone can receive, but there the likeness ends. Insofar as Loman possesses tragic dignity, that eminence derives from his relation to fatherhood. Linda's comment upon her husband—"a small man can be just as exhausted as a great man"—would be an aesthetic disaster if Loman's exhaustion were his salient quality. The exhaustion of Willy Loman simply lacks the cognitive and spiritual qualities that mark the exhaustion of King Lear. Lear and Loman scarcely can be compared without destroying Miller's creation, which makes all the more unfortunate that curious passage in Miller's introduction to his *Collected Plays* in which we are meant to accept the juxtaposition:

> An aged king—a pious man—moves toward life's end. Instead of reaping the benefits of his piety, he finds himself caught in bewildering circumstances. Because of a mistake—an error in judgment—a tragic reversal has taken place in his life. Where he has been priest, knower of secrets, wielder of power, and symbol of life, he now finds himself adjudged defiler, usurper, destroyer, and necessary sacrifice. Like the traditional hero, Loman begins his long season of agony. In his descent, however, there is the familiar tragic paradox; for as he moves toward inevitable destruction, he acquires that knowledge, that sense of reconciliation, which allows him to conceive a redemptive plan for his house.

All that Loman actually shares with Lear or Oedipus is agony; there is no other likeness whatsoever. Miller has little understanding of Classical or Shakespearean tragedy; he stems entirely from Ibsen.

Miller remarks of *Salesman* that it "was written in a mood of friendly partnership with the audience." In reply to an interviewer's question as to whether he was influenced by Jewish tradition, the playwright stressed the Jewish refusal of nihilism:

> Jews can't afford to revel too much in the tragic because it might overwhelm them. Consequently, in most Jewish writing there's always the caution, "Don't push it too far toward the abyss, because you're liable to fall in."

Loman falls in, but is that abyss tragic or pathetic? The answer partly depends upon whether the issue is one of aesthetic dignity, or whether Miller's social sense of tragedy can prevail against traditional canons. Does Loman have enough individuality to sustain the context of tragedy? Again Miller insists upon a social answer:

> ... to me the tragedy of Willy Loman is that he gave his life, or sold it, in order to justify the waste of it. It is the tragedy of a man

who did believe that he alone was not meeting the qualifications laid down for mankind by those clean-shaven frontiersmen who inhabit the peaks of broadcasting and advertising offices. From those forests of canned goods high up near the sky, he heard the thundering command to succeed as it ricocheted down the newspaper-lined canyons of his city, heard not a human voice, but a wind of a voice to which no human can reply in kind, except to stare into the mirror at a failure.

American novelists and American poets have vastly surpassed American playwrights: there is no dramatic William Faulkner or Wallace Stevens to be acclaimed among us. It may be that day-to-day reality in the United States is so violent that stage drama scarcely can compete with the drama of common events and uncommon persons. A wilderness of pathos may be more fecund matter for storyteller and lyricists than it can be for those who would compose tragedies.

Perhaps that is why we value *Death of a Salesman* more highly than its actual achievement warrants. Even half a century back, a universal image of American fatherhood was very difficult to attain. Willy Loman moves us because he dies the death of a father, not of a salesman. Whether Miller's critique of the values of a capitalistic society is trenchant enough to be persuasive, I continue to doubt. But Loman's yearning for love remains poignant, if only because it destroys him. Miller's true gift is for rendering anguish, and his protagonist's anguish authentically touches upon the universal sorrow of failed fatherhood.

Chronology

1915	Born Arthur Asher Miller on October 17 in New York City to Isadore and Augusta ("Gussie") Miller.
1920–28	Attends Public School No. 24 in Harlem.
1923	Sees his first play at the Schubert Theatre.
1928	The Depression causes losses in father's clothing business. Miller family moves to Brooklyn. Has bar mitzvah ceremony at Avenue M Temple.
1933	Graduates from Abraham Lincoln High School. Registers for night school at City College but quits after two weeks.
1934	Begins studies in journalism at the University of Michigan, Ann Arbor.
1936	Writes *No Villain*, a play, in six days and receives Hopwood Award in Drama, from the Avery Hopwood Writing Awards Contest. Switches to studying English.
1937	*They Too Arise*, a rewrite of *No Villain*, is produced in Ann Arbor and Detroit. *Honors at Dawn* receives a Hopwood Award in Drama.
1938	Receives Bachelor of Arts degree. Begins work with the Federal Theater Project in New York to write radio plays and scripts.
1939	Federal Theater is shut down.
1940	Marries Mary Grace Slattery.

1941	Supplements income by working at the Brooklyn Naval Yard as a shipfitter's helper.
1941–47	Writes several radio plays.
1944	Daughter Jane is born on September 7. Visits army camps to garner material for screenplay, *The Story of G.I. Joe*. Publishes *Situation Normal* (prose account of the experience). *The Man Who Had All the Luck* becomes his first play produced on Broadway; wins Theater Guild National Award.
1945	*Focus*, a novel, is published.
1947	*All My Sons* is produced in New York; wins New York Drama Critics' Circle Award. Son Robert is born on May 31.
1949	*Death of a Salesman* opens in Philadelphia and is then produced in New York; wins Pulitzer Prize, New York Drama Critics' Circle Award, Antoinette Perry Award, and many others.
1950	Meets Marilyn Monroe in Hollywood. Adapts Ibsen's *An Enemy of the People*; produced in New York.
1951	First film version of *Death of a Salesman* appears.
1953	*The Crucible* is produced in New York. Receives Antoinette Perry Award.
1955	*A Memory of Two Mondays* and *A View from the Bridge* produced together in New York.
1956	Divorces Mary Grace Slattery in June. Marries Marilyn Monroe. Miller is subpoenaed by the House Un-American Activities Committee. A two-act version of *A View from the Bridge* is produced in London.
1957	Rewrites the short story "The Misfits" into a screenplay for his wife Marilyn to star in. *Arthur Miller's Collected Plays* is published. Convicted of contempt of Congress for refusing to name suspected communists.
1958	Supreme Court reverses his conviction. Miller is elected to the National Institute of Arts and Letters.
1959	Receives Gold Medal for Drama from the National Institute of Arts and Letters.
1961	Divorces Monroe. Film, *The Misfits*, opens in New York.
1962	Marries Austrian-born photographer Inge Morath. Later in the year, Marilyn Monroe is found dead. Son Daniel is born.

1963	Daughter Rebecca is born in September. Children's book, *Jane's Blanket*, is published.
1964	*After the Fall* and *Incident at Vichy* is produced. Miller is elected president of International PEN (Poets, Essayists, and Novelists).
1967	*I Don't Need You Any More*, a collection of short stories, is published. *The Crucible* is produced for television.
1968	*The Price* is produced in New York. The one-millionth copy of *Death of a Salesman* is sold.
1969	*In Russia*, with photographs by Inge Morath, is published.
1970	*Fame* and *The Reason Why*, one-acts, are produced in New York. Miller's works are banned in the Soviet Union as a result of his work to free politically resistant writers.
1971	*A Memory of Two Mondays* and *The Price* appear on television.
1972	*The Creation of the World and Other Business* is produced in New York.
1973	*Incident at Vichy* appears on television.
1974	*Up from Paradise* (musical version of *The Creation of the World and Other Business*) is produced in Michigan. *After the Fall* is produced for television.
1977	*In the Country* is published with Inge Morath. *The Archbishop's Ceiling* is produced in Washington, DC.
1978	*The Theater Essays of Arthur Miller* is published. Miller attends the 25th anniversary of *The Crucible* in Belgium.
1979	*Chinese Encounters* is published with Inge Morath.
1980	*The American Clock* is produced in South Carolina and then New York.
1981	Second volume of *Arthur Miller's Collected Plays* is published.
1982	*Elegy for a Lady* and *Some Kind of Love Story* are produced together in Connecticut.
1983	Directs *Death of a Salesman* in China with Chinese cast.
1984	Receives Kennedy Center Honors for lifetime achievement. *Death of a Salesman* is revived on Broadway with Dustin Hoffman starring as Willy Loman.
1985	*Death of a Salesman* appears on television.

1987   *Danger: Memory!* opens in New York. Publishes autobiography, *Timebends: A Life. All My Sons* is produced on television.

1990   *Everybody Wins*, Miller's screenplay of *Some Kind of Love Story*, opens. *An Enemy of the People* is produced on television.

1991   *The Last Yankee* is produced. *The Ride Down Mt. Morgan* opens in London. *Clara* is produced for television.

1992   *Homely Girl*, a novella, is published.

1993   *The American Clock* appears on television.

1994   *Broken Glass* opens in New York.

1995   *Homely Girl, A Life and Other Stories* is published.

1997   Revised version of *The Ride Down Mt. Morgan* opens in Massachusetts. Film version of *The Crucible* is released.

1998   *Mr. Peter's Connections* premiers. Revival of *A View from the Bridge* wins two Tony Awards. Revised *The Ride Down Mt. Morgan* appears on Broadway. Receives the Senator Claiborne Pell Award for lifetime achievement in the arts.

1999   *Death of a Salesman* is revived on Broadway for 50th anniversary. Wins a Tony Award. Miller is awarded the coveted Dorothy and Lillian Gish Prize.

2000   *The Ride Down Mt. Morgan* appears on Broadway, as well as *The Price. Echoes Down the Corridor*, Miller's essays from 1944 to 2000, is published.

2001   *Untitled*, a previously unpublished one act play written for Vaclav Havel, opens in New York. *Focus* appears as a film. Miller is awarded a National Endowment for the Humanities Fellowship.

2002   Revivals of *The Man Who Had All the Luck* and *The Crucible* play in New York. Inge Morath dies. *Resurrection Blues* opens.

2004   New York revival of *After the Fall. Finishing the Picture* opens.

2005   Arthur Miller dies of heart failure on February 10.

Contributors

HAROLD BLOOM is Sterling Professor of the Humanities at Yale University. He is the author of 30 books, including *Shelley's Mythmaking* (1959), *The Visionary Company* (1961), *Blake's Apocalypse* (1963), *Yeats* (1970), *A Map of Misreading* (1975), *Kabbalah and Criticism* (1975), *Agon: Toward a Theory of Revisionism* (1982), *The American Religion* (1992), *The Western Canon* (1994), and *Omens of Millennium: The Gnosis of Angels, Dreams, and Resurrection* (1996). *The Anxiety of Influence* (1973) sets forth Professor Bloom's provocative theory of the literary relationships between the great writers and their predecessors. His most recent books include *Shakespeare: The Invention of the Human* (1998), a 1998 National Book Award finalist, *How to Read and Why* (2000), *Genius: A Mosaic of One Hundred Exemplary Creative Minds* (2002), *Hamlet: Poem Unlimited* (2003), *Where Shall Wisdom Be Found?* (2004), and *Jesus and Yahweh: The Names Divine* (2005). In 1999, Professor Bloom received the prestigious American Academy of Arts and Letters Gold Medal for Criticism. He has also received the International Prize of Catalonia, the Alfonso Reyes Prize of Mexico, and the Hans Christian Andersen Bicentennial Prize of Denmark.

PETER SZONDI, now deceased, was head of the Institute for General and Comparative Literature at the Free University of West Berlin. He wrote various titles, such as *Essay on the Tragic*.

Professor LEAH HADOMI taught at the University of Haifa in Israel. She is the author of *Elias Canetti or the Failing of the Novel* and has also written on drama and film.

STEVEN R. CENTOLA is Professor of English at Millersville University. He is the editor of Arthur Miller's *Echoes Down the Corridor: Collected Essays, 1944–2000* and *The Achievement of Arthur Miller: New Essays*.

STEPHEN BARKER teaches drama at the University of California, Irvine. He is the author of *Autoaesthetics: Strategies of the Self after Nietzsche* and also has edited titles, such as *Signs of Change: Premodern—Modern—Postmodern*.

CHRISTOPHER BIGSBY is Professor of American Studies at the University of East Anglia, UK. He has published more than 30 books, including *Arthur Miller: A Critical Study*. He edited *The Cambridge Companion to Arthur Miller* and coedited *The Cambridge History of the American Theatre*, a three-volume set. He is the director of the Arthur Miller Centre for American Studies.

COLBY H. KULLMAN is Professor of English at the University of Mississippi. He has been a coeditor on titles, including the three-volume *Studies in American Drama, 1945–Present* and the two-volume *Theatre Companies of the World*.

FRANK ARDOLINO teaches English at the University of Hawaii and specializes in Renaissance literature and drama. He has written two books on Thomas Kyd.

TERRY OTTEN is Professor in the Humanities and Professor of English at Wittenberg University. He has written *After Innocence: Visions of the Fall in Modern Literature* and *The Crime of Innocence in the Fiction of Toni Morrison*.

FRED RIBKOFF has taught at the University of British Columbia and Simon Fraser University. He specializes in the psychological and philosophical implications of tragic literature, how the Holocaust appears in various arts, and American poetry and poetics.

AUSTIN E. QUIGLEY is Professor of English and Comparative Literature at Columbia University and Dean of Columbia College. He has published *Theoretical Inquiry: Language, Linguistics, and Literature* and *The Modern Stage and Other Worlds*.

Bibliography

Ardolino, Frank. "Like Father, Like Sons: Miller's Negative Use of Sports Imagery in *Death of a Salesman*." *Journal of Evolutionary Psychology* 25, nos. 1–2 (March 2004): 32–39.

Bigsby, Christopher. *Arthur Miller and Company*. London: Methuen Drama in association with The Arthur Miller Centre for American Studies, 1990.

———. *A Critical Introduction to Twentieth-Century American Drama 2: Tennessee Williams, Arthur Miller, Edward Albee*. Cambridge: Cambridge University Press, 1984.

———. "Introduction" to *Death of a Salesman: Certain Private Conversations in Two Acts and a Requiem*. New York: Penguin Books, 1998.

———. *Modern American Drama, 1945–1980*. New York: Cambridge University Press, 1992.

Bigsby, Christopher, ed. *Arthur Miller: A Critical Study*. New York: Cambridge University Press, 2005.

———, ed. *The Cambridge Companion to Arthur Miller*. Cambridge: Cambridge University Press, 1997.

Bloom, Harold, ed. *Arthur Miller*. Philadelphia: Chelsea House, 2000.

———. *Arthur Miller's* Death of a Salesman. Philadelphia: Chelsea House, 2004.

———. *Willy Loman*. Philadelphia: Chelsea House, 2005.

Carson, Neil. *Modern Dramatists: Arthur Miller*. New York: St. Martin's Press, 1982.

Centola, Steven R., ed. *The Achievement of Arthur Miller: New Essays*. Dallas: Contemporary Research, 1995.

Cohn, Ruby. "Manipulating Miller." In *Arthur Miller's America: Theater and Culture in a Time of Change*, edited by Enoch Brater, 191–201. Ann Arbor: University of Michigan Press, 2005.

Connolly, Thomas E. "Oedipus, Lear, and Willy Loman." *Hypotheses: Neo-Aristotelian Analysis* 31–32 (Fall 1999–Winter 2000): 9–12.

Cook, Kimberly K. "Valentin and Biff: Each Unhappy in His Own Way?" *Journal of Evolutionary Psychology* 16, nos. 1–2 (March 1995): 47–52.

Dukore, Bernard F. Death of a Salesman *and* The Crucible: *Text and Performance*. Atlantic Highlands, NJ: Humanities Press International, 1989.

Griffin, Alice. *Understanding Arthur Miller*. Columbia: University of South Carolina Press, 1996.

Gussow, Mel, ed. *Conversations with Miller*. New York: Applause, 2002.

Hadomi, Leah. "Fantasy and Reality: Dramatic Rhythm in *Death of a Salesman*." *Modern Drama* 31, no. 2 (June 1988): 157–174.

Hampton, Gregory J. "Black Men Fenced in and a Plausible Black Masculinity," *CLA Journal* 46, no. 2 (December 2002): 194–206.

Harder, Harry. "*Death of a Salesman*: An American Classic." In *Censored Books: Critical Viewpoints*, edited by Nicholas J. Karolides, Lee Burress, and John M. Kean. Metuchen, NJ: Scarecrow Press, 1993, 209–219.

Harksoon, Yim. "Arthur Miller's Theory of Tragedy and Its Practice in *All My Sons*, *Death of a Salesman*, and *The Crucible*." *Publications of the Mississippi Philological Association* (1996): 57–63.

Marino, Stephen A. *"The Salesman Has a Birthday": Essays Celebrating the Fiftieth Anniversary of Arthur Miller's* Death of a Salesman. Lanham, MD: University Press of America, 2000.

Martin, Robert A., ed. *Arthur Miller: New Perspectives*. Englewood Cliffs, NJ: Prentice-Hall, 1982.

———. "The Nature of Tragedy in Arthur Miller's *Death of a Salesman*." *South Atlantic Review* 61, no. 4 (Fall 1996): 97–106.

Martin, Robert A. and Steven R. Centola, eds. *The Theater Essays of Arthur Miller*. New York: Da Capo Press, 1996.

Mason, Jeffrey D. "Paper Dolls: Melodrama and Sexual Politics in Arthur Miller's Early Plays." In *Modern American Drama: The Female Canon*, edited by June Schlueter. Rutherford, N.J.: Fairleigh Dickinson University Press, 1990, pp. 103–115.

Miller, Arthur. *Salesman in Beijing*. New York: Viking Press, 1984.

———. "Unlocking the Secrets of Cultures." *The Drama Review* 47, no. 1 (Spring 2003): 5–7.

Moss, Leonard. Arthur Miller. Boston: G. K. Hall, 1980.

Murphy, Brenda. *Miller, Death of a Salesman*. Cambridge; New York: Cambridge University Press, 1995.

Murphy, Brenda, and Susan C.W. Abbotson. *Understanding Death of a Salesman*. Westport, CT: Greenwood Press, 1999.

Novick, Julius. Death of a Salesman: *Deracination and Its Discontents*. *American Jewish History* 91, no. 1 (March 2003): 97–107.

Oliver, Dominic. "*Arthur Miller's* Death of a Salesman." In *American Writers Classics*, I, edited by Jay Parini. New York: Thomson Gale, 2003, 53–69.

Roudané, Matthew C., ed. *Approaches to Teaching Miller's* Death of a Salesman. New York: The Modern Language Association of America, 1995.

Shaw, Patrick. "The Ironic Characterization of Bernard in *Death of a Salesman*," *Notes on Contemporary Literature* 11, no. 3 (1981): 12.

Shelton, Lewis E. "Elia Kazan and the Psychological Perspective on Directing." *Journal of American Drama and Theatre* 14, no. 3 (Fall 2002): 60–88.

Siebold, Thomas, ed. *Readings on* Death of a Salesman. San Diego, CA: Greenhaven, 1999.

Stanton, Kay. "Women and the American Dream of *Death of a Salesman*." In *Feminist Readings of Modern American Drama*, edited by June Schlueter. Rutherford, NJ: Fairleigh Dickinson University Press, 1989, 67–102.

Stavney, Anne. "Reverence and Repugnance: Willy Loman's Sentiments toward His Son Biff," *Journal of American Drama and Theatre* 4, no. 2 (Spring 1992): 54–62.

Vogel, Dan. "From Milkman to Salesman: Glimpses of the Galut," *Studies in American Jewish Literature* 10, no. 2 (Fall 1991): 172–178.

Welland, Dennis. *Miller, the playwright*. London; New York: Methuen, 1983.

Yoon, So-young. "Willy Loman's Portrait: Trauma of the Absence of the Father," *Journal of Modern British and American Drama* 16, no. 3 (December 2003): 181–209.

Acknowledgments

"Memory: Miller" by Peter Szondi. From *Theory of the Modern Drama*, edited and translated by Michael Hays: pp. 91–95. © 1987 by the University of Minnesota. Reprinted by permission.

"Rhythm Between Fathers and Sons: *Death of a Salesman*" by Leah Hadomi. From *The Homecoming Theme in Modern Drama: The Return of the Prodigal*: pp. 49–62. © 1992 by the Edwin Mellen Press. Reprinted by permission.

"Family Values in *Death of a Salesman*" by Steven R. Centola. From *CLA Journal* 37, no. 1 (September 1993): pp. 29–41. © 1993 by the College Language Association. Reprinted by permission.

"The Crisis of Authenticity: *Death of a Salesman* and the Tragic Muse" by Stephen Barker. Reprinted by permission of the Modern Language Association of American, from *Approaches to Teaching Miller's* Death of a Salesman, edited by Matthew C. Roudané: pp. 82–101. © 1995 by the Modern Language Association of America.

"Arthur Miller: Poet" by Christopher Bigsby. From *Michigan Quarterly Review* 37, no. 4 (Fall 1998): pp. 713–724. © 1998 by the University of Michigan.

"*Death of a Salesman* at Fifty: An Interview with Arthur Miller" by Colby H. Kullman. From *Michigan Quarterly Review* 37, no. 4 (Fall 1998): pp. 624–634. © 1998 by the University of Michigan.

"Miller's Poetic Use of Demotic English in *Death of a Salesman*" by Frank Ardolino. From *Studies in American Jewish Literature* 17 (1998): pp. 120–128. © 1998 by *Studies in American Jewish Literature*.

"*Death of a Salesman*" by Terry Otten. From *The Temptation of Innocence in the Dramas of Arthur Miller*: pp. 26–59. © 2002 by the Curators of the University of Missouri.

"Shame, Guilt, Empathy, and the Search for Identity in Arthur Miller's *Death of a Salesman*" by Fred Ribkoff. From *Modern Drama* 43, no. 1 (Spring 2000): pp. 48–55. Published by the Graduate Centre for the Study of Drama at the University of Toronto and the University of Toronto Press, Inc. © 2000 by the University of Toronto Press, Inc. Reprinted by permission of University of Toronto Press, Inc. www.utpjournals.com.

"Setting the Scene: *Death of a Salesman* and *After the Fall*" by Austin E. Quigley. From *Arthur Miller's America: Theater & Culture in a Time of Change*, edited by Enoch Brater: pp. 60–77. © 2005 by the University of Michigan.

Index